TO SELL IS
HUMAN

Also by Daniel H. Pink

Free Agent Nation
A Whole New Mind
The Adventures of Johnny Bunko
Drive

TO SELL IS HUMAN

THE SURPRISING TRUTH ABOUT PERSUADING, CONVINCING, AND INFLUENCING OTHERS

DANIEL H. PINK

CANONGATE

Edinburgh · London

Published by Canongate Books in 2013

2

Copyright © 2012 by Daniel H. Pink

First published in the United States of America in 2012 by
Riverhead Books, an imprint of Penguin Group (USA) Inc.,
375 Hudson Street, New York, New York 10014, USA

First published in Great Britain in 2013 by Canongate Books Ltd,
14 High Street, Edinburgh EH1 1TE

www.canongate.tv

A portion of Chapter 5 appeared in somewhat
different form in *The Sunday Telegraph*
A portion of Chapter 9 appeared in somewhat
different form in the *Harvard Business Review*

Photographs on pages 69 and 213 by Jessica Lerner
Illustrations on pages 208 and 229–231 by Rob Ten Pas

British Library Cataloguing-in-Publication Data
A catalogue record for this book is available on
request from the British Library

ISBN 978 0 85786 717 9
Export ISBN 978 0 85786 718 6

Book design by Amanda Dewey

Printed and bound in Great Britain by
CPI Group (UK) Ltd, Croydon, CR0 4YY

This book is printed on FSC certified paper

To booksellers, with gratitude

CONTENTS

CONTENTS

Part Three

What to Do

The only thing you got in this world is what you can sell. And the funny thing is, you're a salesman, and you don't know that.

—ARTHUR MILLER,
Death of a Salesman (1949)

Introduction

About a year ago, in a moment of procrastination masquerading as an act of reflection, I decided to examine how I spend my time. I opened my laptop, clicked on the carefully synched, color-coded calendar, and attempted to reconstruct what I'd actually done over the previous two weeks. I cataloged the meetings attended, trips made, meals eaten, and conference calls endured. I tried to list everything I'd read and watched as well as all the face-to-face conversations I'd had with family, friends, and colleagues. Then I inspected two weeks of digital entrails—772 sent e-mails, four blog posts, eighty-six tweets, about a dozen text messages.

When I stepped back to assess this welter of information—a pointillist portrait of what I do and therefore, in some sense, who I am—the picture that stared back was a surprise: I am a salesman.

I don't sell minivans in a car dealership or bound from office to office pressing cholesterol drugs on physicians. But leave aside sleep, exercise, and hygiene, and it turns out that I spend a significant portion of my days trying to coax others to part with resources. Sure, sometimes I'm trying to tempt people to purchase books I've written. But most of what I do doesn't directly make a cash register ring. In that two-week period, I worked to convince a magazine editor to abandon a silly story idea, a prospective business partner to join forces, an organization where I volunteer to shift strategies, even an airline gate agent to switch me from a window seat to an aisle. Indeed, the vast majority of time I'm seeking resources other than money. Can I get strangers to read an article, an old friend to help me solve a problem, or my nine-year-old son to take a shower after baseball practice?

You're probably not much different. Dig beneath the sprouts of your own calendar entries and examine their roots, and I suspect you'll discover something similar. Some of you, no doubt, are selling in the literal sense—convincing existing customers and fresh prospects to buy casualty insurance or consulting services or homemade pies at a farmers' market. But all of you are likely spending more time than you realize selling in a broader sense—pitching colleagues, persuading funders, cajoling kids. Like it or not, we're all in sales now.

And most people, upon hearing this, don't like it much at all.

Sales? *Blecch.* To the smart set, sales is an endeavor that requires little intellectual throw weight—a task for slick glad-handers who skate through life on a shoeshine and a smile. To others it's the province of dodgy characters doing slippery things—a realm where trickery and deceit get the speaking parts while honesty and fairness watch mutely from the rafters. Still others view it as the white-collar equivalent of cleaning toilets—necessary perhaps, but unpleasant and even a bit unclean.

I'm convinced we've gotten it wrong.

This is a book about sales. But it is unlike any book about sales you have read (or ignored) before. That's because selling in all its dimensions—whether pushing Buicks on a car lot or pitching ideas in a meeting—has changed more in the last ten years than it did over the previous hundred. Most of what we think we understand about selling is constructed atop a foundation of assumptions that has crumbled.

In Part One of this book, I lay out the arguments for a broad rethinking of sales as we know it. In Chapter 1, I show that the obituaries declaring the death of the salesman in today's digital world are woefully mistaken. In the United States alone, some 1 in 9 workers still earns a living trying to get others to make a purchase. They may have traded sample cases for smartphones and are offering experiences instead of encyclopedias, but they still work in traditional sales.

More startling, though, is what's happened to the other 8 in 9. They're in sales, too. They're not stalking customers in a furniture showroom, but they—make that *we*—are engaged in what I call "non-sales selling." We're persuading, convincing, and influencing others to give up something they've got in exchange for what we've got. As you'll see in the findings of a first-of-its-kind analysis of people's activities at work, we're devoting upward of 40 percent of our time on the job to moving others. And we consider it critical to our professional success.

Chapter 2 explores how so many of us ended up in the moving business. The keys to understanding this workplace transformation: Entrepreneurship, Elasticity, and Ed-Med. First, Entrepreneurship. The very technologies that were supposed to obliterate salespeople have lowered the barriers to entry for small entrepreneurs and turned more of us into sellers. Second, Elasticity. Whether we work for ourselves or for a large organization, instead of doing only one thing, most of us are finding that our skills on the job must now stretch across boundaries. And as they stretch, they almost always encompass some traditional sales and a lot of non-sales selling. Finally, Ed-Med. The fastest-growing industries around the world are educational services and health care—a sector I call "Ed-Med." Jobs in these areas are all about moving people.

If you buy these arguments, or if you're willing just to rent them for a few more pages, the conclusion might not sit well. Selling doesn't exactly have a stellar reputation. Think of all the movies, plays, and television programs that depict salespeople as one part greedy conniver, another part lunkheaded loser. In Chapter 3, I take on these beliefs—in particular, the notion that sales is largely about deception and hoodwinkery. I'll show how the balance of power has shifted—and how we've moved from a world of *caveat emptor*, buyer beware, to one of *caveat venditor*, seller beware—where honesty, fairness, and transparency are often the only viable path.

That leads to Part Two, where I cull research from the frontiers of social science to reveal the three qualities that are now most valuable in moving others. One adage of the sales trade has long been ABC—"Always Be Closing." The three chapters of Part Two introduce the new ABCs—Attunement, Buoyancy, and Clarity.

Chapter 4 is about "attunement"—bringing oneself into harmony with individuals, groups, and contexts. I draw on a rich reservoir of research to show you the three rules of attunement—and why extraverts rarely make the best salespeople.

Chapter 5 covers "buoyancy"—a quality that combines grittiness of spirit and sunniness of outlook. In any effort to move others, we confront what one veteran salesman calls an "ocean of rejection." You'll learn from a band of life insurance salespeople and some of the world's premier social scientists what to do before, during, and after your sales encounters to remain afloat. And you'll see why actually believing in what you're selling has become essential on sales' new terrain.

In Chapter 6, I discuss "clarity"—the capacity to make sense of murky situations. It's long been held that top salespeople—whether in traditional sales or non-sales selling—are deft at problem *solving*. Here I will show that what matters more today is problem *finding*. One of the most effective ways of moving others is to uncover challenges they may not know they have. Here you'll also learn about the craft of curation—along with some shrewd ways to frame your curatorial choices.

Once the ABCs of Attunement, Buoyancy, and Clarity have taught you how to be, we move to Part Three, which describes what to *do*—the abilities that matter most.

We begin in Chapter 7 with "pitch." For as long as buildings have had elevators, enterprising individuals have crafted elevator pitches. But today, when attention spans have dwindled (and all the people in the elevator are looking at their phones), that technique has become outdated. In this chapter, you'll discover the six successors of the elevator pitch and how and when to deploy them.

Chapter 8, "Improvise," covers what to do when your perfectly attuned, appropriately buoyant, ultra-clear pitches inevitably go awry. You'll meet a veteran improv artist and see why understanding the rules of improvisational theater can deepen your persuasive powers.

Finally comes Chapter 9, "Serve." Here you'll learn the two principles that are essential if sales or non-sales selling are to have any meaning: Make it personal and make it purposeful.

To help you put these ideas into action, at the end of each chapter in Parts Two and Three you'll find dozens of smart techniques assembled from fresh research and best practices around the world. I call these collections of tools and tips, assessments and exercises, checklists and reading recommendations "Sample Cases," in homage to the traveling salesmen who once toted bags bulging with their wares from town to town. By the end of this book, I hope, you will become more effective at moving others.

But equally important, I hope you'll see the very act of selling in a new light. Selling, I've grown to understand, is more urgent, more important, and, in its own sweet way, more beautiful than we realize. The ability to move others to exchange what they have for what we have is crucial to our survival and our happiness. It has helped our species evolve, lifted our living standards, and enhanced our daily lives. The capacity to sell isn't some unnatural adaptation to the merciless world of commerce. It is part of who we are. As you're about to see, if I've moved you to turn the page, selling is fundamentally human.

Part One

Rebirth of a Salesman

1.

We're All in Sales Now

Norman Hall shouldn't exist. But here he is—flesh, blood, and bow tie—on a Tuesday afternoon, sitting in a downtown San Francisco law office explaining to two attorneys why they could really use a few things to spruce up their place.

With a magician's flourish, Hall begins by removing from his bag what looks like a black wand. He snaps his wrist and—voilà!—out bursts a plume of dark feathers. And not just any feathers, he reveals.

"These are . . . Male. Ostrich. Feathers."

This $21.99 feather duster is the best on the market, he tells them in a soft-spoken but sonorous voice. It's perfect for cleaning picture frames, blinds, and any other item whose crevices accumulate dust.

Penelope Chronis, who runs the small immigration firm with her partner in law and in life, Elizabeth Kreher, peers up from her desk and shakes her head. Not interested.

Hall shows her Kitchen Brush #300, a sturdy white and green scrub brush.

They already have one.

Onto Chronis's desk he tosses some "microfiber cloths" and an "anti-fog cloth for car windows and bathroom mirrors."

No thanks.

Hall is seventy-five years old with patches of white hair on the sides of his head and not much in between. He sports conservative eyeglasses and a mustache in which the white hairs have finally overtaken the brown ones after what looks like years of struggle. He wears dark brown pants, a dress shirt with thin blue stripes, a chestnut-colored V-neck sweater, and a red paisley bow tie. He looks like a dapper and mildly eccentric professor. He is indefatigable.

On his lap is a leather three-ring binder with about two dozen pages of product pictures he's clipped and inserted into clear plastic sheets. "This is a straightforward spot remover," he tells Chronis and Kreher when he gets to the laundry page. "These you spray on before throwing something into the washing machine." The lawyers are unmoved. So Hall goes big: moth deodorant blocks. "I sell more of these than anything in my catalog combined," he says. "They kill moths, mold, mildew, and odor." Only $7.49.

Nope.

Then, turning the page to a collection of toilet brushes and bowl cleaners, he smiles, pauses for a perfect beat, and says, "And these are my romantic items."

Still nothing.

But when he gets to the stainless-steel sponges, he elicits a crackle of interest that soon becomes a ripple of desire. "These are wonderful, very unusual. They're scrubber pads, but with a great difference," he says. Each offers eight thousand inches of continuous stainless steel coiled forty thousand times. You can stick them in the dishwasher. A box of three is just $15.

Sold.

Soon he reaches one of his pricier products, an electrostatic carpet sweeper. "It has four terminal brushes made out of natural bristle and nylon. As it goes along the floor, it develops a static current so it can pick up sugar and salt from a bare wood floor," he explains. "It's my favorite wedding gift." Another exquisitely timed pause. "It beats the hell out of a toaster."

Chronis and Kreher go for that, too.

When about twenty minutes have elapsed, and Hall has reached the final sheet in his homemade catalog, he scribbles the $149.96 sale in his order book. He hands a carbon copy of the order to Chronis, saying, "I hope we're still friends after you read this."

He chats for a few moments, then gathers his binder and his bags, and rises to leave. "Thank you very much indeed," he says. "I'll bring everything forthwith tomorrow."

Norman Hall is a Fuller Brush salesman. And not just any Fuller Brush salesman.

He is . . . The. Last. One.

I f you're younger than forty or never spent much time in the United States, you might not recognize the Fuller Brush Man. But if you're an American of a certain age, you know that once you couldn't avoid him. Brigades of salesmen, their sample cases stuffed with brushes, roamed middle-class neighborhoods, climbed the front steps, and announced, "I'm your Fuller Brush Man." Then, offering a free vegetable scrubber known as a Handy Brush as a gift, they tried to get what quickly became known as "a foot in the door."

It all began in 1903, when an eighteen-year-old Nova Scotia farm boy named Alfred Fuller arrived in Boston to begin his career. He was, by his own admission, "a country bumpkin, overgrown and awkward, unsophisticated and virtually unschooled"[1]—and he was promptly fired from his first three jobs. But one of his brothers landed him a sales position at the Somerville Brush and Mop Company—and days before he turned twenty, young Alfred found his calling. "I began without much preparation and I had no special qualifications, as far as I knew," he told a journalist years later, "but I discovered I could sell those brushes."[2]

After a year of trudging door-to-door peddling Somerville products, Fuller began, er, bristling at working for someone else. So he set up a small workshop to manufacture brushes of his own. At night, he oversaw the mini-factory. By day he walked the streets selling what he'd produced. To his amazement, the small enterprise grew. When he needed a few more salespeople to expand to additional products and new territories, he placed an ad in a publication called *Everybody's Magazine*. Within a few weeks, the Nova Scotia bumpkin had 260 new salespeople, a nationwide business, and the makings of a cultural icon.

By the late 1930s, Fuller's sales force had swelled to more than five thousand people. In 1937 alone, door-to-door Fuller dealers gave away some 12.5 million Handy Brushes. By 1948, eighty-three hundred North American salesmen were selling cleaning and hair "brushes to 20 million families in the United States and Canada," according to *The New Yorker*. That same year, Fuller salesmen, all of them independent dealers working on straight commission, made nearly fifty million house-to-house sales calls in the United States—a country that at the time had fewer than forty-three million households. By the early 1960s, Fuller Brush was, in today's dollars, a billion-dollar company.[3]

What's more, the Fuller Man became a fixture in popular culture—Lady Gagaesque in his ubiquity. In the Disney animated version of "The Three Little Pigs," which won an Academy Award in 1933, how did the Big Bad Wolf try to gain entry into the pigs' houses? He disguised himself as a Fuller Brush Man. How did Donald Duck earn his living for a while? He sold Fuller Brushes. In 1948 Red Skelton, then one of Hollywood's biggest names, starred in *The Fuller Brush Man*, a screwball comedy in which a hapless salesman is framed for a crime—and must clear his name, find the culprit, win the girl, and sell a few Venetian blind brushes along the way. Just two years later, Hollywood made essentially the same movie with the same plot—this one called *The Fuller Brush Girl*, with the lead role going to Lucille Ball, an even bigger star. As time went on, you could find the Fuller Brush Man not only on your doorstep, but also in *New Yorker* cartoons, the jokes of TV talk-show hosts, and the lyrics of Dolly Parton songs.

What a Fuller Man did was virtuosic. "The Fuller art of opening doors was regarded by connoisseurs of cold-turkey peddling in somewhat the same way that balletomanes esteem a performance of the Bolshoi—as pure poetry," *American Heritage* wrote. "In the hands of a deft Fuller dealer, brushes became not homely commodities but specialized tools obtainable nowhere else."[4] Yet he[*] was also virtuous, his constant presence in neighborhoods turning him neighborly. "Fuller Brush Men pulled teeth, massaged headaches, delivered babies, gave emetics for poison, prevented suicides, discovered murders, helped arrange funerals, and drove patients to hospitals."[5]

And then, with the suddenness of an unexpected knock on the

---

[*]A Fuller dealer was almost always a "he," although in the 1960s, when the company launched a line of cosmetics, it recruited a group of saleswomen it called Fullerettes.

door, the Fuller Brush Man—the very embodiment of twentieth-century selling—practically disappeared. Think about it. Wherever in the world you live, when was the last time a salesperson with a sample case rang your doorbell? In February 2012, the Fuller Brush Company filed for reorganization under the U.S. bankruptcy law's Chapter 11. But what surprised people most wasn't so much that Fuller had declared bankruptcy, but that it was still around to declare anything.

Norman Hall, however, remains at it. In the mornings, he boards an early bus near his home in Rohnert Park, California, and rides ninety minutes to downtown San Francisco. He begins his rounds at about 9:30 A.M. and walks five to six miles each day, up and down the sharply inclined streets of San Francisco. "Believe me," he said during one of the days I accompanied him, "I know all the level areas and the best bathrooms."

When Hall began in the 1970s, several dozen other Fuller Brush Men were also working in San Francisco. Over time, that number dwindled. And now Hall is the only one who remains. These days when he encounters a new customer and identifies himself as a Fuller Man, he's often met with surprise. "No kidding!" people will say. One afternoon when I was with him, Hall introduced himself to the fifty-something head of maintenance at a clothing store. "Really?" the man cried. "My father was a Fuller Brush salesman in Oklahoma!" (Alas, this prospect didn't buy anything, even though Hall pointed out that the mop propped in the corner of the store came from Fuller.)

After forty years, Hall has a garage full of Fuller items, but his connection to the struggling parent company is minimal. He's on his own. In recent years, he's seen his customers fade, his orders decline, and his profits shrink. People don't have time for a salesman. They want to order things online. And besides, brushes? Who cares? As an accommodation to reality, Hall has cut back the time he devotes to chasing customers. He now spends only two days a week toting his leather binder through San Francisco's retail and business district. And when he unloads his last boar bristle brush and hangs up his bow tie, he knows he won't be replaced. "I don't think people want to do this kind of work anymore," he told me.

Two months after Fuller's bankruptcy announcement, *Encyclopædia Britannica*, which rose to prominence because of its door-to-door salesmen, shut down production of its print books. A month later, Avon—whose salesladies once pressed doorbells from Birmingham to Bangkok—fired its CEO and sought survival in the arms of a corporate suitor. These collapses seemed less startling than inevitable, the final movement in the chorus of doom that, for many years, has been forecasting selling's demise.

The song, almost always invoking Arthur Miller's 1949 play *Death of a Salesman*, goes something like this: In a world where anybody can find anything with just a few keystrokes, intermediaries like salespeople are superfluous. They merely muck up the gears of commerce and make transactions slower and more expensive. Individual consumers can do their own research and get buying advice from their social networks. Large companies can streamline their procurement processes with sophisticated software that pits vendors against one another and secures the lowest price. In the same way that cash machines thinned the ranks of bank tellers and digital switches made telephone operators all but obsolete, today's technologies have rendered salesmen and saleswomen irrelevant. As we rely ever more on websites and smartphones to locate and purchase what we need, salespeople themselves—not to mention the very act of selling—will be swept into history's dustbin.[6]

Norman Hall is, no doubt, the last of his kind. And the Fuller Brush Company itself could be gone for good before you reach the last page of this book. But we should hold off making any wider funeral preparations. All those death notices for sales and those who do it are off the mark. Indeed, if one were to write anything about selling in the second decade of the twenty-first century, it ought to be a birth announcement.

Rebirth of a Salesman (and Saleswoman)

Deep inside a thick semiannual report from the Occupational Employment Statistics program of the U.S. Bureau of Labor Statistics lurks a surprising, and surprisingly significant, piece of data: One out of every nine American workers works in sales.

Each day more than fifteen million people earn their keep by trying to convince someone else to make a purchase.[7] They are real estate brokers, industrial sales representatives, and securities dealers. They sell planes to airlines, trains to city governments, and automobiles to prospective drivers at more than ten thousand dealerships across the country. Some work in posh offices with glorious views, others in dreary cubicles with Dilbert cartoons and a free calendar. But they all sell—from multimillion-dollar consulting agreements to ten-dollar magazine subscriptions and everything in between.

Consider: The United States manufacturing economy, still the largest in the world, cranks out nearly $2 trillion worth of goods each year. But the United States has far more salespeople than factory workers. Americans love complaining about bloated governments—but America's sales force outnumbers the entire federal workforce by more than 5 to 1. The U.S. private sector employs three times as many salespeople as all fifty state governments

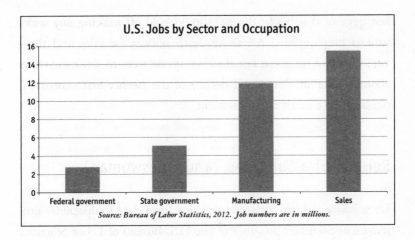

U.S. Jobs by Sector and Occupation

Federal government | State government | Manufacturing | Sales

Source: Bureau of Labor Statistics, 2012. Job numbers are in millions.

combined employ people. If the nation's salespeople lived in a single state, that state would be the fifth-largest in the United States.[8]

The presence of so many salespeople in the planet's largest economy seems peculiar given the two seismic economic events of the last decade—the implosion of the global financial system and the explosion of widespread Internet connectivity. To be sure, sales, like almost every other type of work, was caught in the downdraft of the Great Recession. Between 2006 and 2010, some 1.1 million U.S. sales jobs disappeared. Yet even after the worst downturn in a half-century, sales remains the second-largest occupational category (behind office and administration workers) in the American workforce, just as it has been for decades. What's more, the Bureau of Labor Statistics projects that the United States will add nearly two million *new* sales jobs by 2020. Likewise, the Internet has not had nearly the effect on sales that many predicted. Between 2000 and today, the very period that broadband, smartphones, and e-commerce ascended to disintermediate salespeople and obviate the need for selling, the total number of sales jobs increased and the portion of the U.S. workforce in sales has remained exactly the same: 1 in 9.[9]

What holds for the United States holds equally for the rest of the world. For example, in Canada, "sales and service occupations"—a broader category than the United States uses—constitute slightly more than 25 percent of the Canadian workforce. Australian Bureau of Statistics census data show that about 10 percent of Australia's labor force falls under the heading "sales workers." In the United Kingdom, which uses yet another set of occupation categories, adding up the jobs that involve selling (for example, "sales accounts and business development managers" and "vehicle and parts salespersons or advisers" and so on) totals about three million workers out of a workforce of roughly thirty million—or again, about 1 in 10. In the entire European Union, the figure is slightly higher.[10] According to the most recent available data along with calculations by officials at Eurostat, the EU's statistical agency, about 13 percent of the region's more than two-hundred-million-person labor force works in sales.[11]

Meanwhile, Japan employed nearly 8.6 million "sales workers" in 2010, the last year for which data are available. With almost 63 million people in the total workforce, that means more than 1 out of 8 workers in the world's third-largest economy is in sales.[12] For India and China, larger countries but less developed markets, data are harder to come by. Their portion of salespeople is likely smaller relative to North America, Europe, and Japan, in part because a large proportion of people in these countries still work in agriculture.[13] But as India and China grow wealthier, and hundreds of millions more of their citizens join the middle class, the need for salespeople will inevitably expand. To cite just one example, McKinsey & Company projects that India's growing pharmaceutical industry will triple its cadre of drug representatives to 300,000 employees by 2020.[14]

Taken together, the data show that rather than decline in relevance and size, sales has remained a stalwart part of labor markets around the world. Even as advanced economies have transformed—from hard goods and heavy lifting to skilled services and conceptual thinking—the need for salespeople has not abated.

But that's merely the beginning of the story.

The Rise of Non-Sales Selling

The men and women who operate the world's statistical agencies are among the unsung heroes of the modern economy. Each day they gather bushels of data, which they scrutinize, analyze, and transform into reports that help the rest of us understand what's going on in our industries, our job markets, and our lives. Yet these dedicated public servants are also limited—by budgets, by politics, and, most of all, by the very questions they ask.

So while the idea that 1 in 9 American workers sells for a living might surprise you, I wondered whether it masked a still more intriguing truth. For instance, I'm not a "sales worker" in the categorical sense. Yet, as I wrote in the Introduction, when I sat down to deconstruct my own workdays, I discovered that I spend a sizable portion of them selling in a broader sense—persuading, influencing, and convincing others. And I'm not special. Physicians sell patients on a remedy. Lawyers sell juries on a verdict. Teachers sell students on the value of paying attention in class. Entrepreneurs woo funders, writers sweet-talk producers, coaches cajole players. Whatever our profession, we deliver presentations to fellow employees and make pitches to new clients. We try to convince the boss to loosen up a few dollars from the budget or the human resources department to add more vacation days.

Yet none of this activity ever shows up in the data tables.

The same goes for what transpires on the other side of the ever murkier border between work and life. Many of us now devote a portion of our spare time to selling—whether it's handmade crafts on Etsy, heartfelt causes on DonorsChoose, or harebrained schemes on Kickstarter. And in astonishing numbers and with ferocious energy, we now go online to sell ourselves—on Facebook pages, Twitter accounts, and Match.com profiles. (Remember: None of the six entities I just mentioned existed ten years ago.)

The conventional view of economic behavior is that the two most important activities are producing and consuming. But today, much of what we do also seems to involve *moving*. That is, we're moving other people to part with resources—whether something tangible like cash or intangible like effort or attention—so that we both get what we want. Trouble is, there are no data to either confirm or refute this suspicion—because it involves questions that no statistical agency is asking.

So I set out to fill the void. Working with Qualtrics, a fast-growing research and data analytics company, I commissioned a survey to try to uncover how much time and energy people are devoting to moving others, including what we can think of as non-sales selling—selling that doesn't involve anyone making a purchase.

This study, dubbed the *What Do You Do at Work?* survey, was a comprehensive undertaking. Using some sophisticated research tools, we gathered data from 9,057 respondents around the world. Statisticians at Qualtrics reviewed the responses, disregarded invalid or incomplete surveys, and assessed the sample size and composition to see how well it reflected the population. Because the number of non-U.S. respondents turned out not to be large enough to draw statistically sound conclusions, I've limited much of the analysis to an adjusted sample of more than seven thousand adult full-time workers in the United States. The results have statistical validity similar to those of the surveys conducted by the major opinion research firms that you might read about during election seasons. (For example, Gallup's tracking polls typically sample about 1,000 respondents.)[15]

Two main findings emerged:

1. *People are now spending about 40 percent of their time at work engaged in non-sales selling—persuading, influencing, and convincing others in ways that don't involve anyone making a purchase. Across a range of professions, we are devoting roughly twenty-four minutes of every hour to moving others.*

2. *People consider this aspect of their work crucial to their professional success—even in excess of the considerable amount of time they devote to it.*[*]

Here's a bit more detail about what we found and how we found it:

I began by asking respondents to think about their last two weeks of work and what they did for their largest blocks of time. Big surprise: Reading and responding to e-mail topped the list—followed by having face-to-face conversations and attending meetings.

---

[*]You can find full results of the survey and details on its methodology on my website: http://www.danpink.com/study.

We then asked people to think a bit more deeply about the actual content of those experiences. I presented a series of choices and asked them, "Regardless of whether you were using e-mail, phone, or face-to-face conversations, how much time did you devote to" each of the following: "processing information," "selling a product or a service," and other activities? Respondents reported spending the most time "processing information." But close behind were three activities at the heart of non-sales selling. Nearly 37 percent of respondents said they devoted a significant amount of time to "teaching, coaching, or instructing others." Thirty-nine percent said the same about "serving clients or customers." And nearly 70 percent reported that they spent at least some of their time "persuading or convincing others." What's more, non-sales selling turned out to be far more prevalent than selling in the traditional sense. When we asked how much time they put in "selling a product or service," about half of respondents said "no time at all."

Later in the survey was another question designed to probe for similar information and to assess the validity of the earlier query. This one gave respondents a "slider" that sat at 0 on a 100-point scale, which they could push to the right to indicate a percentage. We asked: *"What percentage of your work involves convincing or persuading people to give up something they value for something you have?"*

The average reply among all respondents: 41 percent. This average came about in an interesting way. A large cluster of respondents reported numbers in the 15 to 20 percent range, while a smaller but significant cluster reported numbers in the 70 to 80 percent range. In other words, many people are spending a decent amount of time trying to move others—but for some, moving others is the mainstay of their jobs. Most of us are movers; some of us are super-movers.

Equally important, nearly everyone considered this aspect of their work one of the most critical components in their professional success. For instance, respondents spent the most time on "processing information." Yet when they listed the tasks that were most vital in doing their job well, they ranked "serving clients and customers" and "teaching, coaching, and instructing others" higher. In addition, even though most people placed "pitching ideas" relatively low on the list of how they allocated their time, more than half of respondents said that this activity was important to their success.

The graph below offers a way to understand the striking interplay between what people find valuable and what they actually do. On the vertical axis is a weighted index, based on survey responses, showing the level of importance assigned to non-sales selling tasks. On the horizontal axis is an index, again based on survey responses, showing how much time people actually spent on these tasks. Bi-

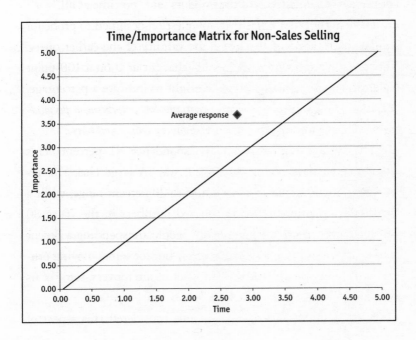

secting the chart on a diagonal is a line indicating a perfect match between time spent and importance. If an activity is plotted below that line, that indicates people are expending time on something that's not commensurately important and presumably should be doing it less. If it's above that line, they're saying that the activity is so critical, they probably should be devoting even more time to it.

Look where non-sales selling falls. It's fairly high on time spent, but even higher on importance. What's more, as demonstrated by the graph below, which breaks out respondents' answers by age groups, the older someone is, and presumably the more experience that person has, the more she says that moving others occupies her days and determines her success.

The *What Do You Do at Work?* survey begins to provide a richer portrait of the twenty-first-century workforce, as exemplified by the world's largest economy. The existing data show that 1 in 9

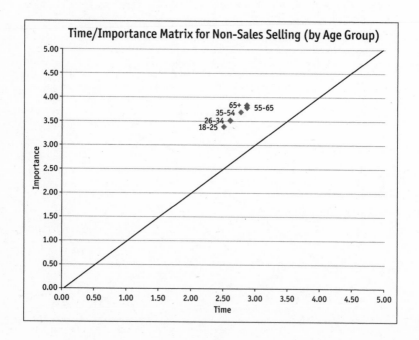

Americans works in sales. But the new data reveal something more startling: So do the other 8 in 9. They, too, are spending their days moving others and depending for their livelihoods on the ability to do it well.

Whether it's selling's traditional form or its non-sales variation, we're all in sales now.

Without fully realizing it, each one of us is doing what Norman Hall has done for nearly half a century and what his Fuller predecessors did for more than a half-century before that. The salesperson isn't dead. The salesperson is alive. Because the salesperson is us.

Which raises a question: How did *that* happen? How did so many of us end up in the moving business?

2.

Entrepreneurship, Elasticity, and Ed-Med

In Chapter 7, you will learn something called the "Pixar pitch." Built on the work of Hollywood's famed animation studio, the technique involves offering a short summary of the point you're trying to make, rendered in the narrative structure of a Pixar film. So, in the hope of modeling behavior I'll later recommend, let me entice you into this chapter with a Pixar pitch.

Once upon a time, only certain people were in sales. Every day, these folks sold stuff, the rest of us did stuff, and everyone was happy. One day, the world began to change. More of us started working for ourselves—and because we were entrepreneurs, suddenly we became salespeople, too. At the same time, large operations discovered that segmenting job functions didn't work very well during volatile business conditions—and because of that, they began demanding elastic skills that stretched across boundaries and included a sales component. Meanwhile, the economy itself transformed so that in the blink of a decade, millions of additional people began working in education and health care—two sectors whose central purpose is moving others. Until finally, in ways we've scarcely realized, most of us ended up in sales.

That's the basic story. To understand it more deeply, let's talk about pickles.

Entrepreneurship

It's easy to poke fun at a place like Brooklyn Brine. The company sells artisanal pickled vegetables (no, really). It's located in Brooklyn. And the people who work there freely use terms like "lavender asparagus," "garlic scape," and "vegan blogger." But ventures like this—one owner, ten employees, fourteen varieties of pickle—are becoming an integral part of the current economy. In the process, they're placing new importance on selling in all its dimensions.

Brooklyn Brine embodies the first of three reasons why more of us find ourselves in sales: the rise of small entrepreneurs.

When we think of the differences between very large enterprises and very small ones, we often focus on differences in degree. The former, by definition, have more revenue, more customers, and more employees. But equally important are differences in *kind*. What people actually do inside tiny operations is often fundamentally different from what they do within massive ones. In particular, large organizations tend to rely on specialization. A two-person company doesn't need a human resources department. A two-thousand-person company can't survive without one. In bigger companies, selling is often a specialized function—a department, a division, a task that some people do so that others can specialize in something else. But proprietors of small operations don't have that luxury. They must wear several hats—often at the same time—and one of these hats is the selling cap.

Shamus Jones, the founder of Brooklyn Brine, calls himself a "reluctant capitalist." He started his career as a chef, grew disenchanted with the restaurant industry, and three years ago ventured out on his own to turn his sometime practice of pickling seasonal vegetables into a full-time business. Without any background in production, operations, or management, he began experimenting with pickle recipes in a restaurateur friend's commercial kitchen from ten at night until eight in the morning. Word spread—you'll now find Brooklyn Brine jars on the shelves of high-end food shops in the United States and Asia—and today Jones spends his time moving product and moving others. He works seven days a week meeting distributors, telling the company's story, and trying to convince stores to stock his wares. When he's back at his factory-cum-storefront, he says his job is to influence employees—so they do their jobs with zeal and with skill. "I want everyone to be happy. I want everyone to be stoked to come into work." He hopes to make money, but that's not the only point. "I want to put out an honest product in an honest company," and that demands traditional selling and non-sales selling in equal measure. Such is the life of a small entrepreneur. Instead of doing one thing, he must do everything. And everything inevitably involves a lot of moving.

To be sure, the world economy includes plenty of planet-straddling behemoths—companies so enormous that they often have more in common with nation-states than with private firms. But the last decade has also witnessed a substantial increase in very small enterprises—not only those like Brooklyn Brine that offer products, but one- or two-person outfits that sell services, creativity, and expertise.

Consider:

- The U.S. Census Bureau estimates that the American economy has more than twenty-one million "non-employer" businesses—operations without any paid employees. These include everything from electricians to computer consultants to graphic designers. Although these microenterprises account for only a modest portion of America's gross domestic product, they now constitute the majority of businesses in the United States.[1]
- The research firm IDC estimates that 30 percent of American workers now work on their own and that by 2015, the number of nontraditional workers worldwide (freelancers, contractors, consultants, and the like) will reach 1.3 billion.[2] The sharpest growth will be in North America, but Asia is expected to add more than six hundred million new soloists in that same period.
- Some analysts project that in the United States, the ranks of these independent entrepreneurs may grow by sixty-five million in the rest of the decade and could become a majority of the American workforce by 2020. One reason is the influence of the eighteen-to-thirty-four-year-old generation as it takes a more prominent economic role. According to research by the Ewing Marion Kauffman Foundation, 54 percent of this age cohort either wants to start their own business or has already done so.[3]
- In sixteen Organisation for Economic Co-operation and Development (OECD) countries—including France, Mexico, and Sweden—more than 90 percent of businesses now have fewer than ten employees. In

addition, the percentage of people who are either a "nascent entrepreneur or owner-manager of a new business" is far higher in markets such as China, Thailand, and Brazil than in the United States or the United Kingdom.[4]

- In our *What Do You Do at Work?* survey, we asked a question designed to probe the issue of micro-entrepreneurship, phrasing it in a way that recognized that many people today earn a living through multiple sources: "Do you work for yourself or run your own business, even on the side?" Thirty-eight percent of respondents answered yes.

Given these numbers, "Instead of rolling our eyes at self-conscious Brooklyn hipsters pickling everything in sight, we might look to them as guides to the future of the . . . economy," says *New York Times Magazine* columnist Adam Davidson.[5] Harvard University's Lawrence Katz, perhaps the top labor economist of his generation, agrees. He projects that middle-class employment of the future won't be employees of large organizations, but self-sufficient "artisans."[6]

Whether we call them artisans, non-employer businesses, free agents, or micro-entrepreneurs, these women and men are selling all the time. They're packaging pickles for customers, of course. But because they're responsible for the entire operation, not merely one facet of it, they're enticing business partners, negotiating with suppliers, and motivating employees. Their industry may be gourmet food or legal services or landscaping—but they're all in the moving business.

One essential—and ultimately ironic—reason for this development: The technologies that were supposed to make salespeople obsolete in fact have transformed more people into sellers. Consider Etsy, an online marketplace for small businesses and craftspeople. Begun with essentially no outside investment in 2005, Etsy now has more than 875,000 active online shops that together sell upward of $400 million of goods each year.[7] Before Etsy came along, the ability of craft makers to reach craft buyers was rather limited. But the Web—the very technology that seemed poised to topple salespeople—knocked down barriers to entry for small entrepreneurs and enabled more of these craft makers to sell. Ditto for eBay. Some three-quarters of a million Americans now say that eBay serves as their primary or secondary source of income.[8] Meanwhile, many entrepreneurs find fund-raising easier thanks to Kickstarter, which allows them to post the basics of their creative projects—films, music, visual art, fashion—and try to sell their ideas to funders. Since Kickstarter launched in 2009, 1.8 million people have funded twenty thousand projects with more than $200 million. In just three years, Kickstarter surpassed the U.S. National Endowment for the Arts as the largest backer of arts projects in the United States.[9]

While the Web has enabled more micro-entrepreneurs to flourish, its overall impact might soon seem quaint compared with the smartphone. As Marc Andreessen, the venture capitalist who in the early 1990s created the first Web browser, has said, "The smartphone revolution is *under*hyped."[10] These handheld minicomputers certainly can destroy certain aspects of sales. Consumers can use them to conduct research, comparison-shop, and bypass salespeople altogether. But once again, the net effect is more creative than destructive. The same technology that renders certain types of salespeople obsolete has turned even more people into potential sellers. For instance, the existence of smartphones has birthed an entire app economy that didn't exist before 2007, when

Apple shipped its first iPhone. Now the production of apps itself is responsible for nearly half a million jobs in the United States alone, most of them created by bantamweight entrepreneurs.[11] Likewise, an array of new technologies, such as Square from one of the founders of Twitter, PayHere from eBay, and GoPayment from Intuit, make it easier for individuals to accept credit card payments directly on their mobile devices—allowing anyone with a phone to become a shopkeeper.

The numbers are staggering. According to MIT's *Technology Review*, "In 1982, there were 4.6 billion people in the world, and not a single mobile-phone subscriber. Today, there are seven billion people in the world—and six billion mobile cellular-phone subscriptions."[12] Cisco predicts that by 2016, the world will have more smartphones (again, handheld minicomputers) than human beings—ten billion in all.[13] And much of the action will be outside North America and Europe, powered "by youth-oriented cultures in . . . the Middle East and Africa."[14] When everyone, not just those in Tokyo and London but also those in Tianjin and Lagos, carries around her own storefront in her pocket—and is just a tap away from every other storefront on the planet—being an entrepreneur, for at least part of one's livelihood, could become the norm rather than the exception. And a world of entrepreneurs is a world of salespeople.

Elasticity

Now meet another guy who runs a company—Mike Cannon-Brookes. His business, Atlassian, is older and much larger than Brooklyn Brine. But what's happening inside is both consistent with and connected to its tinier counterpart.

Atlassian builds what's called "enterprise software"—large, complex packages that businesses and governments use to manage projects, track progress, and foster collaboration among employees. Launched a decade ago by Cannon-Brookes and Scott Farquhar upon their graduation from Australia's University of New South Wales, Atlassian now has some twelve hundred customers in fifty-three countries—among them Microsoft, Air New Zealand, Samsung, and the United Nations. Its revenue last year was $100 million. But unlike most of its competitors, Atlassian collected that entire amount—$100,000,000.00 in sales—*without a single salesperson.*

Selling without a sales force sounds like confirmation of the "death of a salesman" meme. But Cannon-Brookes, the company's CEO, sees it differently. "We have no salespeople," he told me, "because in a weird way, everyone is a salesperson."

Enter the second reason we're all in sales now: Elasticity—the new breadth of skills demanded by established companies.

Cannon-Brookes draws a distinction between "products people buy" and "products people are sold"—and he prefers the former. Take, for instance, how the relationship between Atlassian and its customers begins. In most enterprise software companies, a company salesperson visits potential customers prospecting for new business. Not at Atlassian. Here potential customers typically initiate the relationship themselves by downloading a trial version of one of the company's products. Some of them then call Atlassian's support staff with questions. But the employees who offer support, unlike a traditional sales force, don't tempt callers with fast-expiring discounts or badger them to make a long-term commitment. Instead, they simply help people understand the software, knowing that the value and elegance of their assistance can move wavering buyers to make a purchase. The same goes for engineers. Their job, of course, is to build great software—but that demands more than just slinging code. It also requires discovering customers' needs, understanding how the products are used, and building something so unique and exciting that someone will be moved to buy. "We try to espouse the philosophy that everyone the customer touches is effectively a salesperson," says Cannon-Brookes.

At Atlassian, sales—in this case, traditional sales—isn't anyone's job. It's everyone's job. And that paradoxical arrangement is becoming more common.

Palantir is an even larger company. Based in Palo Alto, California, with offices around the world, it develops software that helps intelligence agencies, the military, and law enforcement integrate and analyze their data to combat terrorism and crime. Although Palantir sells more than a quarter-billion dollars' worth of its software each year, it doesn't have any salespeople either. Instead, it relies on what it calls "forward-deployed engineers." These techies don't create the company's products—at least not at first. They're out in the field, interacting directly with customers and making sure the product is meeting their needs. Ordinarily, that sort of job—handholding the customer, ensuring he's happy—would go to an account executive or someone from the sales division. But Shyam Sankar, who directs Palantir's band of forward-deployed engineers, has at least one objection to that approach. "It doesn't work," he told me.

The more effective arrangement, he says, is "to put real computer scientists in the field." That way, those experts can report back to home-base engineers on what's working and what's not and suggest ways to improve the product. They can tackle the customer's problems on the spot—and, most important, begin to identify new problems the client might not know it has. Interacting with customers around problems isn't selling per se. But it sells. And it forces engineers to rely on more than technical abilities. To help its engi-

neers develop such elasticity, the company doesn't offer sales training or march recruits through an elaborate sales process. It simply
requires every new hire to read two books. One is a nonfiction account of the September 11 attacks, so they're better attuned to what
happens when governments can't make sense of information; the
other is a British drama instructor's guide to improvisational acting, so they understand the importance of nimble minds and lim-
ber skills.*

In short, even people inside larger operations like Atlassian
and Palantir must work more like the shape-shifting pickle-maker
Shamus Jones. This marks a significant change in the way we do
business. When organizations were highly segmented, skills tended
to be fixed. If you were an accountant, you did accounting. You
didn't have to worry about much outside your domain because other
people specialized in those areas. The same was true when business
conditions were stable and predictable. You knew at the beginning
of a given quarter, or even a given year, about how much and what
kind of accounting you'd need to do. However, in the last decade,
the circumstances that gave rise to fixed skills have disappeared.

A decade of intense competition has forced most organizations
to transform from segmented to flat (or at least, flatter). They do the
same, if not greater, amounts of work than before—but they do it
with fewer people who are doing more, and more varied, things.
Meantime, underlying conditions have gone from predictable to
tumultuous. Inventors with new technologies and upstart competitors with fresh business models regularly capsize individual companies and reconfigure entire industries. Research In Motion, maker
of the BlackBerry, is a legend one day and a laggard the next. Retail video rental is a cash cow—until Netflix carves the industry

---

*I'll return to this book, and to the ability to improvise, in Chapter 8.

into flank steak. All the while, the business cycle itself swooshes without much warning from unsustainable highs to unbearable lows like some satanic roller coaster.

A world of flat organizations and tumultuous business conditions—and that's our world—punishes fixed skills and prizes elastic ones. What an individual does day to day on the job now must stretch across functional boundaries. Designers analyze. Analysts design. Marketers create. Creators market. And when the next technologies emerge and current business models collapse, those skills will need to stretch again in different directions.

As elasticity of skills becomes more common, one particular category of skill it seems always to encompass is moving others. Valerie Coenen, for instance, is a terrestrial ecologist for an environmental consulting firm in Edmonton, Alberta. Her work requires high-level and unique technical skills, but that's only the start. She also must submit proposals to prospective clients, pitch her services, and identify both existing and potential problems that she and her firm can solve. Plus, she told me, "You must also be able to sell your services within the company." Or take Sharon Twiss, who lives and works one Canadian province to the west. She's a content strategist working on redesigning the website for a large organization in Vancouver. But regardless of the formal requirements of her job, "Almost everything I do involves persuasion," she told me. She convinces "project managers that a certain fix of the software is a priority," cajoles her colleagues to abide by the site's style guide, trains content providers "about how to use the software and to follow best practices," even works to "get my own way about where we're going for lunch." As she explains, "People who don't have the power or authority from their job title have to find other ways to exert power." Elasticity of skills has even begun reshaping job titles. Timothy Shriver Jr. is an executive at The Future Project, a nonprofit that connects secondary school students with interesting projects to adults who can coach them. His work reaches across different areas—marketing, digital media, strategy, branding, partnerships. But, he says, "The common thread is activating people to move." His title? Chief Movement Officer.

And even those higher on the org chart find themselves stretching. For instance, I asked Gwynne Shotwell, president of the private space transportation firm Space Exploration Technologies Corporation (SpaceX), how many days each week she deals with selling on top of her operational and managerial duties. "Every day," she told me, "is a sales day."

Ed-Med

Larry Ferlazzo and Jan Judson are a husband and wife who live in Sacramento, California. They don't pickle cucumbers or parse code. But they, too, represent the future. Ferlazzo is a high school teacher, Judson a nurse-practitioner—which means that they inhabit the fastest-growing job sector of the United States and other advanced economies.

One way to understand what's going on in the world of work is to look at the jobs people hold. That's what the U.S. Occupational Employment Statistics program, which I cited on page 16, does. Twice a year, it provides an analysis of twenty-two major occupational groups and nearly eight hundred detailed occupations. But another way to understand the current state and future prospects of the workforce is to look at the industries where those jobs emerge. For that, we go to the Monthly Employment Report—and it shows a rather remarkable trend.

The chart on the next page depicts what has happened so far

this century to employment in four sectors—manufacturing, retail trade, professional and business services (which includes law, accounting, consulting, and so on), and education and health services.

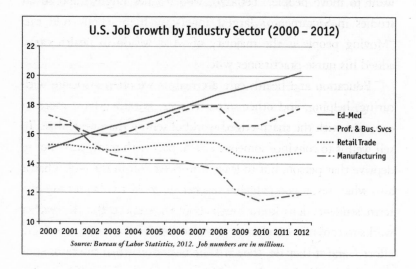

U.S. Job Growth by Industry Sector (2000 – 2012)

— Ed-Med
--- Prof. & Bus. Svcs
···· Retail Trade
-·- Manufacturing

Source: Bureau of Labor Statistics, 2012. Job numbers are in millions.

While jobs in the manufacturing sector have been declining for forty years, as recently as the late 1990s the United States still employed more people in that sector than in professional and business services. About ten years ago, however, professional and business services took the lead. But their ascendance proved short-lived, because rising like a rocket was another sector, education and health services—or what I call Ed-Med. Ed-Med—which includes everyone from community college instructors to proprietors of test prep companies and from genetic counselors to registered nurses—is now, by far, the largest job sector in the U.S. economy, as well as a fast-growing sector in the rest of the world. In the United States, Ed-Med has generated significantly more new jobs in the last decade than all other sectors combined. And over the next decade, forecasters project, health care jobs alone will grow at double the rate of any other sector.[15]

At its core, Ed-Med has a singular mission. "As teachers, we want to move people," Ferlazzo, who teaches English and social studies in Sacramento's largest inner-city high school, told me. "Moving people is the majority of what we do in health care," added his nurse-practitioner wife.

Education and health care are realms we often associate with caring, helping, and other softer virtues, but they have more in common with the sharp-edged world of selling than we realize. To sell well is to convince someone else to part with resources—not to deprive that person, but to leave him better off in the end. That is also what, say, a good algebra teacher does. At the beginning of a term, students don't know much about the subject. But the teacher works to convince his class to part with resources—time, attention, effort—and if they do, they will be better off when the term ends than they were when it began. "I never thought of myself as a sales-man, but I have come to the realization that we all are," says Holly Witt Payton, a sixth-grade science teacher in Louisiana. "I'm sell-ing my students that the science lesson I'm teaching them is the most interesting thing ever," which is something Payton firmly believes. The same is true in health care. For instance, a physical therapist helping someone recover from injury needs that person to hand over resources—again, time, attention, and effort—because doing so, painful though it can be, will leave the patient healthier than if he'd kept the resources to himself. "Medicine involves a lot of salesmanship," says one internist who prefers not to be named. "I have to talk people into doing some fairly unpleasant things."[16]

Of course, teaching and healing aren't the same as selling elec-trostatic carpet sweepers. The *outcomes* are different. A healthy and educated population is a public good, something that is valuable in its own right and from which we all benefit. A new carpet sweeper or gleaming Winnebago, not so much. The *process* can be different, too. "The challenge," says Ferlazzo, "is that to move people a large distance and for the long term, we have to create the conditions where they can move themselves."

Ferlazzo makes a distinction between "irritation" and "agitation." Irritation, he says, is "challenging people to do something that *we* want them to do." By contrast, "agitation is challenging them to do something that *they* want to do." What he has discovered throughout his career is that "irritation doesn't work." It might be effective in the short term. But to move people fully and deeply requires something more—not looking at the student or the patient as a pawn on a chessboard but as a full participant in the game.

This principle of moving others relies on a different set of capabilities—in particular, the qualities of attunement, which I'll explore in Chapter 4, and clarity, which I'll cover in Chapter 6. "It's about leading with my ears instead of my mouth," Ferlazzo says. "It means trying to elicit from people what their goals are for themselves and having the flexibility to frame what we do in that context."

For example, in his ninth-grade class last year, after finishing a unit on natural disasters, Ferlazzo asked his students to write an essay about the natural disaster they considered the very worst. One of his students—Ferlazzo calls him "John"—refused. This wasn't the first time he had done so, either. John had struggled throughout school and had written very little. But he still hoped eventually to graduate.

Ferlazzo told John that he wanted him to graduate, too, but that graduation was unlikely if he couldn't write an essay. "I then told him that I knew from previous conversations that he was on the football team and liked football," Ferlazzo said. "I asked him what his favorite football team was. He looked a little taken aback since it seemed off topic—it looked like he had been expecting a lecture. 'The Raiders,' he replied. Okay, then, what was his least favorite team? 'The Giants.'"

So Ferlazzo asked him to write an essay showing why the Raiders were superior to the Giants. John stayed on task, said Ferlazzo, asked "thoughtful and practical questions," and turned in a "decent essay." Then John asked to write another essay—this one about basketball—to make up for previous essays he hadn't bothered to do. Ferlazzo said yes. John delivered another pretty good piece of written work.

"Later that week, in a parent-teacher conference with all of his teachers, John's mother cried when I showed her the two essays. She said he'd never written one before" during his previous nine years of schooling.

Ferlazzo says he "used agitation to challenge him on the idea of graduating from high school and I used my ears knowing that he was interested in football." Ferlazzo's aim wasn't to force John to write about natural disasters but to help him develop writing skills. He convinced John to give up resources—ego and effort—and that helped John move himself.

Ferlazzo's wife—the Med to his Ed—sees something similar with her patients. "The model of health care is 'We're the experts.' We go in and tell you what to do." But she has found, and both experience and evidence confirm, that this approach has its limits. "We need to take a step back and bring [patients] on board," she told me. "People usually know themselves way better than I do." So now, in order to move people to move themselves, she tells them,

"I need your expertise." Patients heal faster and better when they're part of the moving process.

Health care and education both revolve around non-sales selling: the ability to influence, to persuade, and to change behavior while striking a balance between what others want and what you can provide them. And the rising prominence of this dual sector is potentially transformative. Since novelist Upton Sinclair coined the term around 1910, and sociologist C. Wright Mills made it widespread forty years later, experts and laypeople alike have talked about "white-collar" workers. But now, as populations age and require more care and as economies grow more complex and demand increased learning, a new type of worker is emerging. We may be entering something closer to a "white coat/white chalk" economy,[17] where Ed-Med is the dominant sector and where moving others is at the core of how we earn a living.

D oes all of this mean that you, too, are in the moving business—that entrepreneurship, elasticity, and Ed-Med have unwittingly turned you into a salesperson? Not necessarily. But you can find out by answering the following four questions:

1. **Do you earn your living trying to convince others to purchase goods or services?**

    If you answered yes, you're in sales. (But you probably knew that already.) If you answered no, go to question 2.

2. **Do you work for yourself or run your own operation, even on the side?**

    If yes, you're in sales—probably a mix of traditional sales and non-sales selling. If no, go to question 3.

3. **Does your work require elastic skills—the ability to cross boundaries and functions, to work outside your specialty, and to do a variety of different things throughout the day?**

   If yes, you're almost certainly in sales—mostly non-sales selling with perhaps a mix of traditional sales now and then. If no, go to question 4.

4. **Do you work in education or health care?**

   If yes, you're in sales—the brave new world of non-sales selling. If no, and if you answered no to the first three questions, you're not in sales.

So where did you end up? My guess is that you found yourself where I found myself—living uneasily in a neighborhood you might have thought was for someone else. My guess, too, is that this makes you uncomfortable. We've seen movies like *Glengarry Glen Ross* and *Tin Men,* which depict sales as fueled by greed and founded on misdeed. We've been cornered by the fast-talking commissioned salesman urging us to sign on the line that is dotted. Sales—even when we give it a futuristic gloss like "non-sales selling"—carries a seamy reputation. And if you don't believe me, turn to the next chapter so I can show you a picture.

3.

From *Caveat Emptor* to *Caveat Venditor*

What do people really think of sales? To find out, I turned to an effective, and often underused, methodology: I asked them. As part of the *What Do You Do at Work?* survey, I posed the following question to respondents: *When you think of "sales" or "selling," what's the first word that comes to mind?*

The most common answer was *money*, and the ten most frequent responses included words like "pitch," "marketing," and "persuasion." But when I combed through the list and removed the nouns, most of which were value-neutral synonyms for "selling," an interesting picture emerged.

What you see on page 45 is a word cloud. It's a graphic representation of the twenty-five adjectives and interjections people offered most frequently when prompted to think of "sales" or "selling," with the size of each word reflecting how many respondents used it. For instance, "pushy" was the most frequent adjective or interjection (and the fourth-most-mentioned word overall), thus its

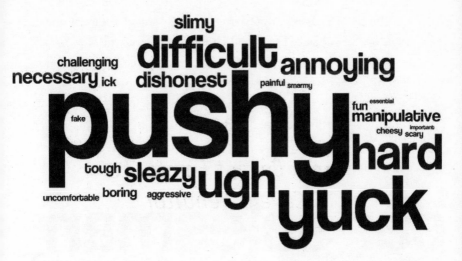

impressive size. "Smarmy," "essential," and "important" are tinier because they were mentioned less often.

Adjectives and interjections can reveal people's attitudes, since they often contain an emotional component that nouns lack. And the emotions elicited by "sales" or "selling" carry an unmistakable flavor. Of the twenty-five most offered words, only five have a positive valence ("necessary," "challenging," "fun," "essential," and "important"). The remainder are all negative. These negative words assemble into two camps. A few reflect people's *discomfort* with selling ("tough," "difficult," "hard," "painful"), but most reflect their *distaste*. Words like "pushy" and "aggressive" figure prominently, along with a batch of adjectives that suggest deception: "slimy," "smarmy," "sleazy," "dishonest," "manipulative," and "fake."

This word cloud, a linguistic MRI of our brains contemplating sales, captures a common view. Selling makes many of us uncomfortable and even a bit disgusted ("ick," "yuck," "ugh"), in part because we believe that its practice revolves around duplicity, dissembling, and double-dealing.

To probe people's impressions further, I asked a related question, one better suited to visual thinkers: *When you think of "sales" or "selling," what's the first picture that comes to mind?* (Respondents had to describe their picture in five or fewer words.)

To my surprise, the responses—in overwhelming numbers—took a distinct form. They involved a man in a suit selling a car, generally a used one. Take a look at the resulting word cloud for the twenty-five most popular answers:

car salesman

aggressive telephone — sleazy extrovert shark — money

professional door to door salesman **slick** tie outgoing **smile** man talker annoying **used car car** handshake

used car salesman

pushy briefcase **man in a suit**

suit

The top five responses, by a wide margin, were: "car salesman," "suit," "used-car salesman," "man in a suit," and our old friend, "pushy." (The top ten also included both "car" and "used car" on their own.) The image that formed in respondents' minds was uniformly male. The word "man" even made the top twenty-five. Very few people used the gender-neutral term "salesperson" and nobody answered "saleswoman." Many respondents emphasized the sociable aspects of sales—with "outgoing," "extrovert," and "talker" all making the top twenty-five. Others settled on more metaphorical or literary images, including "shark" and "Willy Loman." And some people still couldn't resist offering adjectives: "slick," "sleazy," and "annoying."

It turns out that these two word clouds, taken together, can help us puncture one of the most pervasive myths about selling in all its forms. The beliefs embedded in that first image—that sales is distasteful because it's deceitful—aren't so much inherently wrong as they are woefully outdated. And the way to understand that is by pulling back the layers of that second image.

Lemons and Other Sour Subjects

In 1967, George Akerlof, a first-year economics professor at the University of California, Berkeley, wrote a thirteen-page paper that used economic theory and a handful of equations to examine a corner of the commercial world where few economists had dared to tread: the used-car market. The first two academic journals where young Akerlof submitted his paper rejected it because they "did not publish papers on topics of such triviality."[1] The third journal also turned down Akerlof's study, but on different grounds. Its reviewers didn't say his analysis was trivial; they said it was mistaken. Finally, two years after he'd completed the paper, *The Quarterly Journal of Economics* accepted it and in 1970 published "The Market for 'Lemons': Quality Uncertainty and the Market Mechanism." Akerlof's article went on to become one of the most cited economics papers of the last fifty years. In 2001, it earned him a Nobel Prize.

In the paper, Akerlof identified a weakness in traditional economic reasoning. Most analyses in economics began by assuming that the parties to any transaction were fully informed actors making rational decisions in their own self-interest. The burgeoning field of behavioral economics has since called into question the second part of that assumption—that we're all making rational decisions in our own self-interest. Akerlof took aim at the first part—that we're fully informed. And he enlisted the used-car market for what he called "a finger exercise to illustrate and develop"[2] his ideas.

Cars for sale—he said, oversimplifying in the name of clarifying—fall into two categories: good and bad. Bad cars, what Americans call "lemons," are obviously less desirable and therefore ought to be cheaper. Trouble is, with used cars, only the seller knows whether the vehicle is a lemon or a peach. The two parties confront "an asymmetry in available information."[3] One side is fully informed; the other is at least partially in the dark.

Asymmetrical information creates all sorts of headaches. If the seller knows much more about the product than the buyer, the buyer understandably gets suspicious. What's the seller concealing? Am I being hoodwinked? If the car is so great, why is he getting rid of it? As a result, the buyer might be willing to pay only very little—or perhaps forgo purchasing the car altogether. But Akerlof theorized that the problems could ripple further. Suppose I've got a used car that I know is a peach, and I decide to sell it. Buyers still treat me the same way they treat any seller—as a presumptive lemon peddler. What's this guy Pink keeping secret? Is he bamboozling us? If the car is so peachy, why is he unloading it? One consequence is that as the seller, I settle for a price lower than the auto is worth. The other is that I give up and don't even bother trying to sell my car. "Dishonest dealings tend to drive honest dealings out of the market," Akerlof wrote. "The presence of people who wish to pawn bad wares as good wares tends to drive out the legitimate business." And it's not just autos, he said. The same reasoning applies to insurance, credit, or one's own labor. When honest sellers opt out, the only ones who remain are the shysters and the charlatans—pushy guys in suits using sleazy tactics to stick you with a heap of junk. *Ick.*

Of course, individuals and institutions have devised ways to make Akerlof's commercial landscape less forbidding. Sellers offer warranties on their goods. Brand names provide some assurance of quality. Legislatures pass "lemon laws" to protect consumers. But most important, prospective purchasers are on notice. When sellers know more than buyers, buyers must beware. It's no accident that people in the Americas, Europe, and Asia today often know only two words of Latin. In a world of information asymmetry, the guiding principle is *caveat emptor*—buyer beware.

Akerlof's provocative thought piece recast how economists and others reckoned with individual transactions and entire markets. So with this example as a model, let's try another intellectual finger exercise. Imagine a world not of information asymmetry, but of something closer to information parity, where buyers and sellers have roughly equal access to relevant information. What would happen then? Actually, stop imagining that world. You're living in it.

Go back to used cars. In the United States today, a prospective purchaser of, say, a used Nissan Maxima can arm herself with all manner of relevant information before even approaching a seller. She can go online and find most of the places offering that particular car within a certain radius of her home, thereby giving her a wider set of choices. She can tap her social network or visit websites to discover each dealer's reputation and whether previous customers have been satisfied. For individual sellers, she can spend fifteen minutes on a search engine checking the person's bona fides. She can visit online forums to see what current Maxima owners think of the car. She can check Kelley Blue Book, Edmunds, or

AutoTrader.com to find out the price used Maximas are going for. And once she sees a car she likes, she can take the auto's Vehicle Identification Number and, with a quick online search, find out whether it's been in accidents or had major repairs. She's not fully protected from unethical sellers, of course. But if she encounters any dirty dealing, or ends up dissatisfied, she can do more than simply gripe to a neighbor. She can tell a few hundred Facebook friends, all her Twitter followers, and the readers of her blog—some of whom may pass her story on to their own networks, undermining the seller's ability to deceive again. Now extend the realities of the market for used cars to the market for just about anything else.

Buyers today aren't "fully informed" in the idealized way that many economic models assume. But neither are they the hapless victims of asymmetrical information they once were. That's why that first word cloud isn't wrong. It's just out of date. The belief that sales is slimy, slick, and sleazy has less to do with the nature of the activity itself than with the long-reigning but fast-fading conditions in which selling has often taken place.

The balance has shifted. If you're a buyer and you've got just as much information as the seller, along with the means to talk back, you're no longer the only one who needs to be on notice. In a world of information parity, the new guiding principle is *caveat venditor*—seller beware.

Finding Your Kowalskis

Joe Girard might as well have parachuted down from that second word cloud, ready to do whatever it takes to put you in a Chevy Malibu this afternoon. He is the world's greatest salesman. I know because he told me. Then he sent me a few pages from *Guinness World Records* testifying to his achievement and confirmed by a major accounting firm. In one year, he sold 1,425 cars at Merollis Chevrolet in Detroit. These weren't fleet sales either. These were one-at-a-time, belly-to-belly sales—several cars every day for an entire year. It's a remarkable achievement.

So how did he do it?

His book, *How to Sell Anything to Anybody*—whose cover claims "2 million copies in print!"—reveals the secrets, which he also shares with live audiences around the world. "I guarantee you that my system will work for you, if you understand and follow it," he promises.[4]

The centerpiece is "Girard's Rule of 250"—that each of us has 250 people in our lives we know well enough to invite to a wedding or a funeral. If you reach one person, and get her to like you and buy from you, she will connect you to others in her 250-person circle. Some of those people will do the same. And so on and so on in ever-widening cascades of influence. Girard advises us to "fill the seats on the Ferris wheel" with as many prospects as we can, to let them off the Ferris wheel for a while after they buy, and then to turn them into your "birddogs" by paying them $50 for every new sale they subsequently send you. "A Chevrolet sold by Joe Girard is not just a car," he writes. "It is a whole relationship between me and the customer and his family and friends and the people he works with."[5]

Alas, many of the techniques Girard recommends to establish that relationship invite the unsavory adjectives of that first word cloud. For instance, if prospects mention they've recently been on vacation somewhere, Girard will say that he's been there, too. "Because wherever that guy has been, I have been. Even if I never heard of the place," he writes. "A lot of people out there, maybe millions, have heard of me. And thousands have bought from me. They think they know a lot about me, because I know a lot about them. They think I have been to Yellowstone National Park. They think I have fished for salmon near Traverse City, Michigan. They think I have an aunt who lives near Selfridge Air Force base."[6] Take your pick: "dishonest," "smarmy," or "ugh."

Girard also describes in three lengthy but glorious paragraphs one of his favorite tactics for cold-calling prospective customers. It begins by choosing a name from the phone book and placing a call.

> Now a woman answers the phone. "Hello, Mrs. Kowalski. This is Joe Girard at Merollis Chevrolet. I just wanted to let you know that the car you ordered is ready," I tell her. Now remember: this is a cold call, and all I know for sure from the phone book is the party's name, address, and phone number. This Mrs. Kowalski doesn't know what I'm talking about. "I'm afraid you have the wrong number. We haven't ordered a new car," she tells me. "Are you sure?" I ask. "Pretty sure. My husband would have told me," she says. "Just a minute," I say. "Is this the home of Clarence J. Kowalski?" "No. My husband's name is Steven." . . . "Gee, Mrs. Kowalski, I'm very sorry to have disturbed you at this hour of the day. I'm sure you're very busy."

But Girard doesn't let her go. He keeps her talking so he can bait the hook.

> "Mrs. Kowalski, you don't happen to be in the market for a new car, do you?" If she knows they are, she'll probably

say yes. But the typical answer will be: "I don't think so, but you have to ask my husband." There it is, what I'm looking for. "Oh, when can I reach him?" And she'll say, "he's usually home by 6." Okay, I got what I wanted. "Well, fine, Mrs. Kowalski, I'll call back then, if you're sure I won't be interrupting supper." I wait for her to tell me they don't eat until about six-thirty, and then I thank her.

From there, Girard moves to the next stage.

You know what I am going to be doing at six o'clock. That's right. "Hello, Mr. Kowalski, this is Joe Girard at Merollis Chevrolet. I spoke to Mrs. Kowalski this morning and she suggested I call back at this time. I was wondering if you are in the market for a new Chevrolet?" "No," he says, "not just yet." So I ask, "Well, when do you think you might start looking at a new car?" I ask the question straight out, and he is going to think about it and give me an answer. Maybe he only wants to get rid of me. But whatever the reason what he says is probably going to be what he really means. It's easier than trying to dream up a lie. "I guess I'll be needing one in about 6 months," he says, and I finish with: "Fine, Mr. Kowalski. I'll be getting in touch with you then. Oh, by the way, what are you driving now?" He tells me, I thank him, and hang up.[7]

Girard files Mr. Kowalski's name, along with a reminder in his calendar to call him, and moves to the next name on this list. "After the easy ones," Girard writes, "there are many Kowalskis, if you keep searching."[8]

That Girard found enough clueless Kowalskis to become the world's greatest salesman—and that he remains out and about teaching sales skills—might seem to validate that information asymmetry and the ignoble tactics it allows are alive and well. But there's one more thing you should know about Joe Girard. He hasn't actually sold a car since 1977. He quit the business more than three decades ago to teach others how to sell. (The Deloitte & Touche audit his office sent me verifying his record is dated 1991 and covers a fifteen-year period beginning in 1963.) Girard's techniques might have gleamed in the mid-1970s. But in the mid-2010s, they have the whiff of old boxes forgotten in the attic. After all, these days, Mrs. Kowalski is at work. Her household has caller ID to prevent telephonic intrusions. And if a salesman did circumvent her family's defenses, she would dispatch him quickly, maybe Google his name afterward, and tell her Facebook friends about the creepy call she received that night.

When I reached Girard by phone one afternoon[*] to ask how the world of sales had changed since he last commanded the showroom, he insisted that it hadn't. The effect of the Internet? "That is junk. I don't need that crap," he told me. Now that consumers have ample access to information, how does that alter the sales process? "Not at all. There's only one way. My way." Could he be as successful on today's landscape as he was in the 1970s? "Give me nine months and I'll rule the world."

To be fair, much of what Girard advocates remains sensible and enduring. He's a staunch advocate of service after the sale. "Service, service, service," he told me during our conversation. He offers one of the clearest aphorisms on effective selling I've heard: "Peo-

---

[*] Girard and his office declined several requests for a face-to-face interview.

ple want a fair deal from someone they like." But more broadly, his worldview and his tactics resemble one of those old movies in which a soldier stuck on a remote island continues fighting because he hasn't gotten word that the war has ended.

Contrast that to Tammy Darvish. When Girard was selling Chevys in Detroit, Darvish was in primary school. Now she's vice president of DARCARS Automotive Group, one of the largest auto dealers on the East Coast. If her home is any indication, the car business has been very good to her. The fifteen-thousand-square-foot manor where I sat down with her one afternoon contains a foyer that could double as an awesome basketball court. Darvish has dark hair that falls just past her shoulders. She's petite, friendly, and semi-intense, though the intense part seems natural and the semi- an effort. Nobody in the survey pictured *her* when they conjured an image of sales.

Darvish came to the industry the old-fashioned way: Her father owned automobile dealerships in the Washington, D.C., area. After graduating from Northwood University in Midland, Michigan, with a degree in automotive marketing, she began at the bottom, a junior sales consultant facing scorching skepticism. She was a twenty-year-old woman—the boss's daughter, no less—in a heavily male field. In her first month, she outsold her peers and was named "salesman" of the month. Then she did it again in month two. A career was born.

Nearly thirty years later, she has watched the decline of information asymmetry reshape her business. In the old days, customers drove from dealership to dealership collecting what intelligence they could. "Today most of that is done before they show up. And in many cases they are more educated than we are," she said. "When I graduated from college, the factory invoice of a car was locked in a safe. We didn't know the cost [of the cars we were sell-ing]. Today, the customer is telling me."

When buyers can know more than sellers, sellers are no longer protectors and purveyors of information. They're the curators and clarifiers of it—helping to make sense of the blizzard of facts, data, and options. "If a customer has any question at all," Darvish told me, "I can say, 'Let's go to Chevy.com'" and figure out the answer together.

She acknowledges that "when you go into a car dealer, you expect a plaid jacket and polyester pants." But just as those ques-tionable fashion choices have become outmoded, so have the skeezy practices they conjure. Indeed, much of what we believe about sales derives not from the inherent nature of selling but from the infor-mation asymmetry that long defined the context in which people sold. Once that asymmetry diminishes, and the seesaw rebalances, everything gets upended. For example, DARCARS has an unusual policy of rarely hiring experienced salespeople, who might have learned bad habits or acquired old-school perspectives. Likewise, Darvish believes that many sales training programs are "a little mechanical," that they risk turning people into selling robots who recite memorized scripts on cue and try to steamroll customers into decisions. "We bring them in and we put them in a one-week training course that's not just about sales. We talk about customer service and social media."

Most of all, what makes someone effective on this shifted ter-rain is different from the smooth-talking, backslapping, pocket-picking stereotype of the past. Darvish says the qualities she looks for most are persistence—and something for which a word never appeared in either of the word clouds: empathy.

"You can't train someone to care," she told me. To her the ideal salespeople are those who ask themselves, "What decision would I make if that were my own mom sitting there trying to get service or buy a car?" It sounds noble. And maybe it is. But today, it's how you sell cars.

Joe Girard is a reason why we had to live by *caveat emptor.* Tammy Darvish survives—and thrives—because she lives by *caveat venditor.*

The decline of information asymmetry hasn't ended all forms of lying, cheating, and other sleazebaggery. One glimpse of the latest financial shenanigans from Wall Street, the City, or Hong Kong confirms that unhappy fact. When the product is complicated—credit default swaps, anyone?—and the potential for lucre enormous, some people will strive to maintain information imbalances and others will opt for outright deception. That won't change. As long as flawed and fallible human beings walk the planet, *caveat emptor* remains useful guidance. I heed this principle. So should you. But the fact that some people will take the low road doesn't mean that lots of people will. When the seller no longer holds an information advantage and the buyer has the means and the opportunity to talk back, the low road is a perilous path.

Caveat venditor extends well beyond car sales to refashion most encounters that involve moving others. Take travel. In the old days—that is, fifteen years ago—travel agents maintained an information monopoly that allowed the unscrupulous ones to overcharge and mistreat their customers. Not anymore. Today, a mom with a laptop has about the same access to airfares, hotel rates, and reviews as a professional. Or consider selling yourself for a job. You can no longer control all the information about yourself, some of which you selectively include in your sales document, the résumé. Today, a company might still look at that résumé but, as CNN notes, the company will also "browse your LinkedIn and Facebook profiles, read the gory details in your blog and hit Google to find out more about you—good or bad—all in one sitting."[9]

The new rules of *caveat venditor* also govern the booming Ed-Med sector. Today, it's possible for a motivated secondary school student with Internet access to know more about the causes of the Peloponnesian War or how to make a digital film than his teacher. Physicians, once viewed as imperial dispensers of specialized knowledge, now might see patients who've researched their ailment and arrive with a clutch of studies and a course of action. Today's educators and health care professionals can no longer depend on the quasi-reverence that information asymmetry often afforded them. When the balance tilts in the opposite direction, what they do and how they do it must change. Ed-Med, beware.

A Tale of Two Saturdays

Steve Kemp is a man in a suit who sells used cars. His business, SK Motors ("Where everybody rides!") in Lanham, Maryland, sits on a colorless patch of Maryland State Route 564, down the road from a roller rink and Grace Baptist Church. Kemp is an old-fashioned businessman—a cheerful fellow, ruddy and heavyset, who belongs to the local Rotary Club and whose service shop offers free detailing to the teacher of the month at a neighborhood school. And SK Motors is an old-fashioned place. Its inventory of about fifty used cars—from a Mercedes-Benz SL to a Hyundai Elantra—sits in an asphalt lot ringed with starter flags. At the edge is a compact one-story, five-room structure that serves as the office.

One sunny Saturday morning, two salesmen, Frank and Wayne, sip coffee in the front room, waiting for the first customer on what is always the busiest day of the week. Frank is a soft-spoken African-American man who's seventy-four years old but looks fifty-five. He's been selling cars since 1985. Wayne is about the same age, white and cantankerous, with a baseball cap and plaid shirt.

Onto the lot drives a chain-smoking man in a parka and his rail-thin twenty-something son, who sports a valiant attempt at a beard and a jacket that bears the name of the local electric utility. The younger man needs a car. He admires the three-year-old Nissan Altima but can't afford its $16,500 price. So he goes for the 1993 Ford Escort with 117,000 miles. With Frank in the front seat, he takes the car for a test drive. Then they return to the front room to make a deal.

He fills out a credit application. Steve's right-hand man, Jimmy, takes the application and heads to his office, which houses one of the company's two computers, to do a credit check. Whammo. The report reads like a rap sheet. The young customer has had collection actions aplenty. He's also had cars repossessed, including one he purchased from SK Motors. Frank summons Steve. They confer briefly and Steve enters the room.

"We're now at the *woodyaiff* stage," he whispers to me.

Huh?

"*Would you if* we did this? *Would you if* we did that?" he whispers again.

Steve is willing to offer a loan—at SK's standard interest rate of 24 percent and with a tracking device attached to the car—if the young man makes a $1,500 down payment. *Woodyaiff* those were the terms? The man doesn't have any money for a down payment. He leaves.

Two more customers come in, neither serious.

In the midst of lunch, a tall man wearing a cowboy hat and jacket emblazoned with Jack Daniel's logos arrives. He's looking for a cheap car—everyone who comes in is—and finds a burnt-orange Acura for $3,700. He and Frank do a test drive. When they return, he's ready to buy. Frank doesn't say much. He just doesn't get in the way. They bargain the price down to $3,200—and the man in the cowboy hat drives off. It's one P.M. and SK Motors has its first sale of the day.

By two P.M., Wayne is asleep at his desk.

At about four P.M., Steve sells a 2003 Dodge Stratus with 70,000 miles to a woman who needs a car for her teenage son. By the time we close up shop that evening, SK Motors has sold two cars.

On another Saturday, I head to another used-car lot—a CarMax auto superstore in Rockville, Maryland. It's about thirty miles away from SK Motors in distance and light-years in form. This place has more cars in the *customer* parking lot than SK had for sale. Its collection of vehicles spans a block-sized stretch of asphalt that looks like an airport parking lot—complete with sections designated by letters to help people find their way. Inside the main office, the place is buzzing like a low-wattage stock market floor—two dozen desks, more than forty salespeople, customers galore.

But the biggest difference isn't size or noise. It's information. At SK Motors that Saturday, not a single customer seemed to have done even the most rudimentary research on prices, competing deals, or car quality in advance of the visit. Here about half the customers are clutching printouts they've brought from home. Others are pecking at their smartphones and iPads. And those who still need access can use a bank of computers CarMax has made available. SK Motors, which serves customers whose options are limited and whose credit is so compromised they'll tolerate monitoring devices and sky-high interest rates, can still benefit from information asymmetry. CarMax has built its business model around the opposite.

The company launched in 1993 hoping to reinvent the way Americans bought used cars. Two decades later, CarMax is a Fortune 500 company that sells more than four hundred thousand vehicles each year and collects annual revenue of more than $9 billion.[10] From the start, it tried to undo the conventions that gave rise to that first word cloud. For instance, it established a set price for each car—no haggling necessary. That reduces a customer's fear of being outbargained by a more informed seller. Also, CarMax salespeople—most of them decked in blue polo shirts with a company logo rather than a suit and tie—earn their pay entirely through commissions. But those commissions aren't based on the price of the car. Selling a budget car earns the same commission as selling an expensive one. That mitigates the fear that a pushy salesman will press you to buy a vehicle that's good for his wallet rather than yours. Finally, CarMax practically disgorges information. Since any customer on her own can find a report on the vehicle's condition or history, CarMax gives that to customers for free. It offers warranties, certifications, and guarantees to address the quality concerns that Akerlof identified back in 1967.

But the sharpest example is in plain view when you walk into the store. Each salesperson sits at a small desk—him on one side, the customer on the other. Each desk also has a computer. In most settings, the seller would look at the computer screen and the buyer at the computer's backside. But here the computer is positioned not in front of either party, but off to the side with its screen facing outward so both buyer and seller can see it at the same time. It's the literal picture of information symmetry.

No haggling. Transparent commissions. Informed customers. Once again, it all sounds so enlightened. And maybe it is. But that's not why this new approach exists.

This is why: On the Saturday I spent at SK Motors, a total of eight customers came in the entire day. On the Saturday at Car-Max, more than that showed up in the first fifteen minutes.

As we've seen, *caveat venditor* has become just as important as *caveat emptor*. Whether you're in traditional sales or non-sales selling, the low road is now harder to pass and the high road—honesty, directness, and transparency—has become the better, more pragmatic, long-term route.

Yet the idea that we're all in sales still rests uneasily for some people, in part because of a few other myths I'll quickly address here.

The first is the myth of the blockhead. "We do not seem to have gone much in for genius," wrote Fuller Brush Company founder Alfred Fuller of his sales force.[11] The way this myth has it, the smarties go off to become engineers and lawyers, while those consigned to the less favorable portions of the IQ bell curve distribution migrate toward sales, which requires far less cognitive horsepower.* Not quite. As you'll see in Parts Two and Three of this book, when simple, transactional tasks can be automated, and when information parity displaces information asymmetry, moving people depends on more sophisticated skills and requires as much intellect and creativity as designing a house, reading a CT scan, or, say, writing a book.

The second erroneous belief, and a reason that some people disdain sales, is the myth of the moneygrubber: that being effective requires being greedy and that the best (and perhaps only) way

---

*One brilliant example of this view is the comic strip *Dilbert* and its recurring character "Kenny the Sales Weasel." In one episode, he and Dilbert go off to meet the company's biggest prospect. As they climb into the car, Kenny says, "Tell me all of our product's technical specs on the way. I like to be prepared." Dilbert replies, "Our product is beige. It uses electricity." "Whoa!" cries Kenny. "Brain overload!"

to succeed is to become a coin-operated selling machine. Once again, not quite. For starters, non-sales selling, especially in domains such as Ed-Med, has nothing to do with cash. And considerable research has shown that money is not the driving force even for the majority of people in traditional sales.[12] What's more, as you'll read in the Sample Case at the end of Chapter 9, a number of companies have actually increased sales by *eliminating* commissions and *de-emphasizing* money.

Finally, many people—myself included until I began researching this book—believe the myth of the natural. Some people have sales chops. Others don't. Some people are innately skilled at moving others. The rest of us are out of luck. Here we confront a paradox. There are no "natural" salespeople, in part because we're *all* naturally salespeople. Each of us—because we're human—has a selling instinct, which means that anyone can master the basics of moving others. The rest of this book will show you how.

Part Two

How to Be

4.

Attunement

In the 1992 movie *Glengarry Glen Ross*, based on David Mamet's Pulitzer Prize– and Tony Award–winning play of the same name, four small-time salesmen inhabit the seedy Chicago office of a real estate company called Mitch and Murray. They've been struggling lately, these salesmen. So on a gloomy, rain-soaked night, the downtown bosses dispatch Blake, a cold-blooded predator in a well-tailored suit, to kick them into higher gear.

In one of the epic scenes in the cinema of sales, Blake, played by a young Alec Baldwin, schools the middle-aged men on how to sell. His instruction begins with derision, as he questions their masculinity and pelts them with profanities. From there, he moves to fear. "We're adding a little something to this month's sales contest," he says. "As you all know, first prize is a Cadillac Eldorado. Anybody want to see second prize?" He holds up a package. "Second prize's a set of steak knives." He pauses. "Third prize is you're fired. You get the picture?"

Blake then concludes his harangue with some old-fashioned

sales training, flipping over a green chalkboard and pointing to where he's written the first three letters of the alphabet. "A-B-C," he explains. "A—always. B—be. C—closing. Always be closing. Always be closing."

"Always be closing" is a cornerstone of the sales cathedral. Successful salespeople, like successful hunters of any species, never relent in pursuing their prey. Every utterance and each maneuver must serve a single goal: pushing the transaction to a conclusion—your conclusion—and getting the person across the table, as Blake says, "to sign on the line which is dotted."

Always be closing. Its simplicity makes it understandable; its alphabeticality makes it memorable. And it can be constructive advice, keeping sellers focused on a deal's end even during its beginning and middle. But the effectiveness of this advice is waning because the conditions on which it depends are fading. When only some of us are in sales—and when buyers face minimal choices and information asymmetry—"Always be closing" is sensible counsel. But when all of us are in sales, and none of us has much of an information edge, Blake's prescription seems as dated as the electric typewriters and Rolodex cards that dot Mitch and Murray's office.

Remapped conditions require revamped navigation. So here in Part Two, I introduce the new ABCs of moving others:

A—*Attunement*
B—*Buoyancy*
C—*Clarity*

Attunement, buoyancy, and clarity: These three qualities, which emerge from a rich trove of social science research, are the new requirements for effectively moving people on the remade landscape of the twenty-first century. We begin in this chapter with A—Attunement. And to help you understand this quality, let me get you thinking about another letter.

Power, Empathy, and Chameleons

Take a moment right now—and if there's someone in the room with you, politely request thirty seconds of his or her time. Then ask that person to do the following: "First, with your dominant hand, snap your fingers five times as quickly as you can. Then, again as quickly as you can, use the forefinger of your dominant hand to draw a capital E on your forehead." Seriously, go ahead and do this. I'll wait. (If you're alone, slip this exercise in your back pocket and pull it out at your next opportunity.)

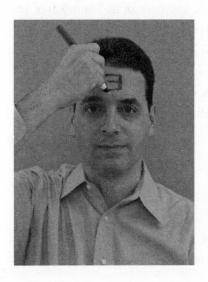 

Now look at the way your counterpart drew his or her E. Which photograph on the previous page does it look like?

The difference might seem innocuous, but the letter on your counterpart's forehead offers a window into his mind. If the E resembles the one on the left, the person drew it so he could read it himself. If it looks likes the one on the right, he drew the E so *you* could read it.

Since the mid-1980s, social psychologists have used this technique—call it the E Test—to measure what they dub "perspective-taking." When confronted with an unusual or complex situation involving other people, how do we make sense of what's going on? Do we examine it from only our own point of view? Or do we have "the capability to step outside [our] own experience and imagine the emotions, perceptions, and motivations of another?"[1]

Perspective-taking is at the heart of our first essential quality in moving others today. Attunement is the ability to bring one's actions and outlook into harmony with other people and with the context you're in. Think of it as operating the dial on a radio. It's the capacity to move up and down the band as circumstances demand, locking in on what's being transmitted, even if those signals aren't immediately clear or obvious.

The research shows that effective perspective-taking, attuning yourself with others, hinges on three principles.

1. Increase your power by reducing it.

In a fascinating study a few years ago, a team of social scientists led by Adam Galinsky at Northwestern University's Kellogg School of Management probed the relationship between perspective-taking and power. They divided their participants into two groups, the only difference being what each experienced immediately before the key experiment. One group completed a series of exercises that induced feelings of power. The other did a different set of activities designed to emphasize their lack of power.

Then researchers gave the people in each group the E Test. The results were unmistakable: "High-power participants were almost three times as likely as low-power participants to draw a self-oriented 'E.'"[2] In other words, those who'd received even a small injection of power became less likely (and perhaps less able) to attune themselves to someone else's point of view.

Now try another test on yourself, one that doesn't require anybody's forehead. Imagine that you and your colleague Maria go out to a fancy restaurant that's been recommended by Maria's friend Ken. The experience is awful. The food stinks, the service is worse. The following day Maria sends Ken an e-mail that says only, "About the restaurant, it was marvelous, just marvelous." How do you think Ken will interpret the comment? Will he consider the e-mail sincere or sarcastic? Think about it for a moment before reading further.

In a related experiment, Galinsky and his crew used a version of this scenario to examine power and perspective-taking from another angle—and found results similar to what they uncovered with the E Test. Participants with high power generally believed that Ken found the e-mail sarcastic; those with low power predicted he found it sincere. Who's correct? Chances are, it's the low-power group. Remember: Ken has no idea what happened at the dinner. Unless Maria is a chronically sarcastic person, of which there was no evidence in the experiment, Ken has no reason to suspect insincerity on the part of his friend. To conclude that he inferred sarcasm in Maria's e-mail depends on "privileged background knowledge" that Ken doesn't have. As the researchers conclude, "power leads individuals to anchor too heavily on their own vantage point, insufficiently adjusting to others' perspective."[3]

The results of these studies, part of a larger body of research, point to a single conclusion: an inverse relationship between power and perspective-taking. Power can move you off the proper position on the dial and scramble the signals you receive, distorting clear messages and obscuring more subtle ones.

This is a hugely important insight for understanding how to move others. The ability to take another's perspective mattered less when sellers—whether a commissioned salesperson in an electronics store or a physician in her diploma-studded office—held all the cards. Their edge in information—again, whether that information was the reliability of a clock radio or the experiences of patients with Lyme disease—gave them the ability to command through authority and sometimes even to coerce and manipulate. But as that information advantage has withered, so has the power it once conferred. As a result, the ability to move people now depends on power's inverse: understanding another person's perspective, getting inside his head, and seeing the world through his eyes. And doing that well requires beginning from a position that would get you expelled from the Mitch and Murray always-be-closing school of sales: Assume that you're *not* the one with power.

Research by Dacher Keltner at the University of California, Berkeley, and others has shown that those with lower status are keener perspective-takers. When you have fewer resources, Keltner explained in an interview, "you're going to be more attuned to the context around you."[4] Think of this first principle of attunement as persuasion jujitsu: using an apparent weakness as an actual strength. Start your encounters with the assumption that you're in a position of lower power. That will help you see the other side's perspective more accurately, which, in turn, will help you move them.

Don't get the wrong idea, though. The capacity to move others doesn't call for becoming a pushover or exhibiting saintly levels of selflessness. Attunement is more complicated than that, as the second principle is about to demonstrate.

2. Use your head as much as your heart.

Social scientists often view perspective-taking and empathy as fraternal twins—closely related, but not identical. Perspective-taking is a cognitive capacity; it's mostly about thinking. Empathy is an emotional response; it's mostly about feeling. Both are crucial. But Galinsky, William Maddux at INSEAD business school in Fontainebleau, France, and two additional colleagues have found that one is more effective when it comes to moving others.

In a 2008 experiment, the researchers simulated a negotiation over the sale of a gas station. Like many real-life negotiations, this one presented what looked like an obstacle: The highest price the buyer would pay was less than the lowest price the seller would accept. However, the parties had other mutual interests that, if surfaced, could lead to a deal both would accept. One-third of the negotiators were instructed to imagine what the other side was *feeling*, while one-third was instructed to imagine what the other side was *thinking*. (The remaining third, given bland and generic instructions, was the control group.) What happened? The empathizers struck many more deals than the control group. But the perspective-takers did even better: 76 percent of them managed to fashion a deal that satisfied both sides.

Something similar happened in another negotiation situation, this one involving a set of thornier and more conflicting issues between a recruiter and a job candidate. Once again, the perspective-takers fared best, not only for themselves but also for their negotiation partners. "Taking the perspective of one's opponent produced both greater joint gains and more profitable individual outcomes. . . . Perspective takers achieved the highest level of economic efficiency, without sacrificing their own material gains," Galinsky and Maddux wrote. Empathy, meanwhile, was effective but less so "and was, at times, a detriment to both discovering creative solutions and self-interest."[5]

Traditional sales and non-sales selling often involve what look like competing imperatives—cooperation versus competition, group gain versus individual advantage. Pushing too hard is counterproductive, especially in a world of *caveat venditor*. But feeling too deeply isn't necessarily the answer either—because you might submerge your own interests. Perspective-taking seems to enable the proper calibration between the two poles, allowing us to adjust and attune ourselves in ways that leave both sides better off. Empathy can help build enduring relationships and defuse conflicts. In medical settings, according to one prominent physician, it is "associated with fewer medical errors, better patient outcomes, more satisfied patients . . . fewer malpractice claims and happier doctors."[6] And empathy is valuable and virtuous in its own right. But when it comes to moving others, perspective-taking is the more effective of these fraternal twins. As the researchers say, ultimately it's "more beneficial to get inside their heads than to have them inside one's own heart."[7]

This second principle of attunement also means recognizing that individuals don't exist as atomistic units, disconnected from groups, situations, and contexts. And that requires training one's perspective-taking powers not only on people themselves but also on their relationships and connections to others. An entire field of study, social network analysis, has arisen in the last fifteen years to reveal these connections, relationships, and information flows.[8] In most sales situations, however, we don't have the luxury of the deep research and fancy software that social network analysts use. So we must rely less on GPS-style directions—and more on our intuitive sense of where we are. In the world of waiters and waitresses, this sort of attunement is called "having eyes" or "reading a table." It allows the server to quickly interpret the group dynamics and adjust his style accordingly. In the world of moving others, I call this ability "social cartography." It's the capacity to size up a situation and, in one's mind, draw a map of how people are related.

"I do this in every sales situation," says Dan Shimmerman, founder of Varicent Software, a blazingly successful Toronto company recently acquired by IBM. "For me it's very important to not just have a good understanding of the key players involved in making a decision, but to understand what each of their biases and preferences are. The mental map gives a complete picture, and allows you to properly allocate time, energy and effort to the right relationships." Social cartography—drawing that map in your head—ensures that you don't miss a critical player in the process, Shimmerman says. "It would stink to spend a year trying to sell Mary only to learn that Dave was the decision maker."

Nonetheless, attunement isn't a merely cognitive exercise. It also has a physical component, as our third principle of attunement will show.

3. Mimic strategically.

Human beings are natural mimickers. Without realizing it, we often do what others do—mirroring back their "accents and speech patterns, facial expressions, overt behaviors, and affective responses."[9] The person we're talking to crosses her arms; we do the same. Our colleague takes a sip of water; so do we. When we notice such imitation, we often take a dim view of it. "Monkey see, monkey do," we sniff. We smirk about those who "ape" others' behavior or "parrot" back their words as if such actions somehow lie beneath human dignity. But scientists view mimicry differently. To them, this tendency is deeply human, a natural act that serves as a social glue and a sign of trust. Yet they, too, assign it a nonhuman label. They call it the "chameleon effect."[10]

In an award-winning study, Galinsky and Maddux, along with Stanford University's Elizabeth Mullen, tested whether mimicry deepened attunement and enhanced the ability to move others. They used the same scenarios as in the previous study—the gas station sale and the negotiation between a job hunter and a recruiter—but added a new dimension. Five minutes before the exercise began, some of the participants received an "important message" that gave them additional instructions for carrying out their assignment:

> Successful negotiators recommend that you should mimic the mannerisms of your negotiation partner to get a better deal. For example, when the other person rubs his/her face, you should, too. If he/she leans back or leans forward in the chair, you should, too. However, they say *it is very important that you mimic subtly enough that the other person does not notice what you are doing*, otherwise this technique completely backfires. Also, do not direct too much of your attention to the mimicking so you don't lose focus on the outcome of the negotiation. Thus, you should find a happy medium of consistent but subtle mimicking that does not disrupt your focus.[11] (Emphasis in the original.)

"Strategic mimicry" proved to be effective. The participants told to mimic—again, with just five minutes of notice and preparation—did it surprisingly well and to great effect. In the gas station scenario, "negotiators who mimicked their opponents' mannerisms were more likely to create a deal that benefited both parties."[12] In the recruiting scenario, the mimickers fared better than the non-mimickers—and did so without adversely affecting the other side. The researchers titled their paper, "Chameleons Bake Bigger Pies and Take Bigger Pieces."[13]

The reasons, Galinsky explains, go to our very roots as a species. Our brains evolved at a time when most of the people around us were those we were related to and therefore could trust. But "as the size of groups increased, it required more sophisticated understandings and interactions with people," he told an interviewer. People therefore looked to cues in the environment to determine whom they could trust. "One of those cues is the unconscious awareness of whether we are in synch with other people, and a way to do that is to match their behavioral patterns with our own."[14] Synching our mannerisms and vocal patterns to someone else so that we both understand and can be understood is fundamental to attunement.

Other research demonstrates mimicry's effectiveness. For example, a Dutch study found that waitresses who repeated diners' orders word for word earned 70 percent more tips than those who paraphrased orders—and that customers with servers who mimicked were more satisfied with their dining experience.[15] In a French study of retail salespeople, half of the store clerks were instructed to mimic the expressions and nonverbal behavior of their customers and half were not. When customers approached the salespeople for help, nearly 79 percent bought from mimickers compared with about 62 percent from non-mimickers. In addition, those who dealt with the mimickers reported "more positive evaluations of both the sales clerk and the store."[16] A Duke University experiment in which an interviewer presented what purported to be a new sport drink found that when people were subtly mimicked, they were more likely to say they would buy the drink and to predict that it would be a success.[17]

And much as perspective-taking and empathy are fraternal twins, mimicry has a first cousin: touching. The research here, much of it by French social psychologist Nicolas Guéguen, is similarly plentiful. For instance, several studies have shown that when restaurant servers touch patrons lightly on the arm or shoulder, diners leave larger tips.[18] One of Guéguen's studies found that women in nightclubs were more likely to dance with men who lightly touched their forearm for a second or two when making the request. The same held in a non-nightclub setting, when men asked for women's phone numbers.[19] (Yes, both studies took place in France.) In other research, when signature gatherers asked strangers to sign a petition, about 55 percent of people did so. But when the canvassers touched people once on the upper arm, the percentage jumped to 81 percent.[20] Touching even proved helpful in our favorite setting: a used-car lot. When salesmen (all the sellers were male) lightly touched prospective buyers, those buyers rated them far more positively than they rated salespeople who didn't touch.[21]

Of course, mimicry, like the other attunement behaviors, requires deftness. When people know they're being mimicked, which was exceedingly rare in the experiments, it can have the opposite effect, turning people against you.[22] Twisting the dial toward someone else's perspective doesn't mean claiming that you've been to the place where your prospect just vacationed or that your uncle lives in her hometown. That's not attunement. That's lying. The key is to be strategic *and* human—to be strategic *by* being human.

Gwen Martin understands that. She began her career as a salesperson and in 2007 cofounded NumberWorks, a staffing agency headquartered in Minneapolis that provides accountants and financial professionals to organizations that need help with complex projects. The company is one of the fastest-growing in its industry, and one reason, I had heard, was Martin's sales prowess.

So on a trip to Minnesota, and in a subsequent phone interview, I asked her what qualities were necessary in effectively moving others. At the time, I'd not yet encountered the research above. She knew nothing of it either. Martin surprised me by repeatedly using a word one rarely hears in this context: "humility." "The most common thread in the people who are really good at this is humility," she told me. "They take the attitude of 'I'm sitting in the small chair so you can sit in the big chair.'" That's perspective-taking through reducing power, the first rule of attunement.

Martin also said that top salespeople have strong emotional intelligence but don't let their emotional connection sweep them away. They are curious and ask questions that drive to the core of what the other person is thinking. That's getting into their heads and not just their hearts, attunement rule number two.

Most of all, "you have to be able somehow to get in synch with people, to connect with them, whether you're with a grandmother or the recent graduate of an MBA program," she told me.

How does she describe this capacity?

"This might sound strange," she said, "but I call it the ability to chameleon."

The Ambivert Advantage

Extraverts make the best salespeople. The reasons are clear from the very textbook definition of this personality type: "Individuals high on extraversion are characterized as sociable, assertive, lively, and sensation seeking."[23] Moving others requires interacting with others—and social situations, which can drain the energy of introverts, is something extraverts relish. Extraverts' comfort with other people also means they don't shrink from making requests, and such assertiveness helps, whether you're convincing a prospective client to hire your public relations firm or asking a stranger to switch seats on a train. Extraverts are friendly and gregarious, which means they're more likely to strike up the lively conversations that lead to relationships and ultimately, perhaps, to sales. Finally, extraverts, by their very nature, seek stimulation, and the energy and enthusiasm that bubble up can be infectious, not to mention conducive to many forms of influence and persuasion. Sociable, assertive, lively, and sensation-seeking: It's the ideal profile for moving others.

"Salespeople represent the prototypical extraverts in our culture," many analysts say, the very embodiment of "the extravert ideal" that shapes Western society.[24] Little wonder, then, that extraverts often pursue careers in sales, that most sales guides extol outgoingness and sociability, or that research confirms that managers select for this trait when hiring a sales force.[25]

The notion that extraverts are the finest salespeople is so obvious that we've overlooked one teensy flaw. There's almost no evidence that it's actually true.

When social scientists have investigated the relationship between extraversion and sales success, they've found the link, at best, flimsy. For instance, while supervisors often give extraverts high *ratings*, several researchers have found that extraversion has "no statistically significant relationship . . . with sales *performance*" and that "extraversion is not related to sales *volume*."[26] One of the most comprehensive investigations—a set of three meta-analyses of thirty-five separate studies involving 3,806 salespeople—found that the correlation between extraversion and sales was essentially nonexistent. (Positive correlations are measured on a scale that goes from 0 to 1, with higher numbers—say, 0.62—indicating close correlations and 0 no correlation at all. Across the thirty-five studies, the correlation between extraversion and sales performance was a minuscule 0.07.)[27]

Does this mean that introverts—those soft-spoken souls more at home in a study carrel than at a cocktail party—are better at moving others? Not at all. In fact, the evidence, which is emerging in new research, reveals something far more intriguing.

Adam Grant is a management professor at the University of Pennsylvania's Wharton School and one of America's top young social psychologists. Some of his previous research had examined extraversion[28] and he'd become curious that a trait so widely associated with sales didn't have much connection to success in that realm. So he decided to find out why.

Grant collected data from a software company that operates call centers to sell its products. He began by asking more than three hundred sales representatives to complete several personality assessments, including one that social scientists use to measure where people fall on the introversion-extraversion spectrum. This particular assessment lists statements such as "I am the life of the party" and "I am quiet around strangers" and asks participants to rate themselves on a 1-to-7 scale, with their answers resulting in a numerical measure of extraversion. Then Grant tracked the sales representatives' revenues over the next three months.[29]

Perhaps not surprisingly, introverted sales reps didn't perform as well as extraverted ones, earning an average of $120 per hour in revenue compared with $125 per hour for their more outgoing colleagues. But neither did nearly as well as a third group: the ambiverts.

Ambi-whats?

These are people who are neither overly extraverted nor wildly introverted.[30] Go back to that 1-to-7 introversion-extraversion scale. Ambiverts sit roughly in the center. They're not 1s or 2s, but they're not 6s or 7s. In Grant's study, these Goldilocks personalities—not too hot, not too cold—earned an average of nearly $155 per hour, easily besting their counterparts. In fact, the salespeople who had the highest average revenue—$208 per hour—had extraversion scores of 4.0, smack at the midpoint.

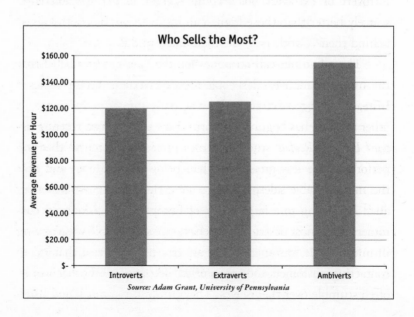

Who Sells the Most?

Source: Adam Grant, University of Pennsylvania

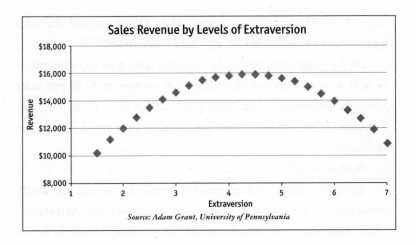

Source: Adam Grant, University of Pennsylvania

What's more, when Grant plotted total revenue over the three months against employees' scores on the 1-to-7 scale, he found a distinct, and revealing, pattern. Indeed, revenue peaked between 4 and 4.5—and fell off as the personality moved toward either the introvert or extravert pole. Those highest in extraversion fared scarcely better than those highest in introversion, but both lagged behind their coworkers in the modulated middle.[31]

"These findings call into question the longstanding belief that the most productive salespeople are extraverted," Grant writes.[32] Instead, being too extraverted can actually impair performance, as other research has begun to confirm. For example, two recent *Harvard Business Review* studies of sales professionals found that top performers are less gregarious than below-average ones and that the most sociable salespeople are often the poorest performers of all.[33] According to a large study of European and American customers, the "most destructive" behavior of salespeople wasn't being ill-informed. It was an excess of assertiveness and zeal that led to contacting customers too frequently.[34] Extraverts, in other words, often stumble over themselves. They can talk too much and listen too little, which dulls their understanding of others' perspectives. They can fail to strike the proper balance between asserting and holding back, which can be read as pushy and drive people away.*

The answer, though, isn't to lurch to the opposite side of the spectrum. Introverts have their own, often reverse, challenges. They can be too shy to initiate and too timid to close. The best approach is for the people on the ends to emulate those in the center. As some have noted, introverts are "geared to inspect," while extraverts are "geared to respond."[35] Selling of any sort—whether traditional sales or non-sales selling—requires a delicate balance of inspecting and responding. Ambiverts can find that balance. They know when to speak up and when to shut up. Their wider repertoires allow them to achieve harmony with a broader range of people and a more varied set of circumstances. Ambiverts are the best movers because they're the most skilled attuners.

For most of you, this should be welcome news. Look again at the shape of the curve in that second chart. That's pretty much what the distribution of introverts and extraverts looks like in the wider population.[36] A few of us are extraverts. A few of us are introverts. But most of us are ambiverts, sitting near the middle, not the edges, happily attuned to those around us. In some sense, we are born to sell.

---

*One of the few sales pros who picked up on this long ago was Fuller Brush Company founder Alfred Fuller. "Previously I had imagined the salesman as a talker who could charm a doorknob into buying brass polish," he wrote in his memoirs. However, "The Fuller Brush Man is not often the extrovert of the cartoons. . . . More often than not, he is rather shy, masking this trait with studied confidence."

SAMPLE CASE

•————————————•

Attunement

Discover the best way to start a conversation.

Everything good in life—a cool business, a great romance, a powerful social movement—begins with a conversation. Talking with each other, one to one, is human beings' most powerful form of attunement. Conversations help us understand and connect with others in ways no other species can.

But what's the best way to start a conversation—especially with someone you don't know well? How can you quickly put the person at ease, invite an interaction, and build rapport?

For guidance, look to Jim Collins, author of the classic *Good to Great* and other groundbreaking business books. He says his favorite opening question is: *Where are you from?*

The wording allows the other person to respond in a myriad of ways. She might talk in the past tense about location ("I grew up in Berlin"), speak in present tense about her organization ("I'm from Chiba Kogyo Bank"), or approach the question from some other angle ("I live in Los Angeles, but I'm hoping to move").

This question has altered my own behavior. Because I enjoy hearing about people's experiences at work, I often ask people: *What do you do?* But I've found that a few folks squirm at this because they don't like their jobs or they believe that others might pass judgment. Collins's question is friendlier and more attuned. It opens things up rather than shuts them down. And it always triggers an interesting conversation about something.

Practice strategic mimicry.

Gwen Martin says that what makes some salespeople extraordinary is their "ability to chameleon"—to adjust what they do and how they do it to others in their midst. So how can you teach yourself to be a bit more like that benevolent lizard and begin to master the techniques of strategic mimicry?

The three key steps are *Watch*, *Wait*, and *Wane*:

1. **Watch.** Observe what the other person is doing. How is he sitting? Are his legs crossed? His arms? Does he lean back? Tilt to one side? Tap his toe? Twirl his pen? How does he speak? Fast? Slow? Does he favor particular expressions?

2. **Wait.** Once you've observed, don't spring immediately into action. Let the situation breathe. If he leans back, count to fifteen, then consider leaning back, too. If he makes an important point, repeat back the main idea verbatim—but a bit later in the conversation. Don't do this too many times, though. It's not a contest in which you're piling up points per mimic.

3. **Wane.** After you've mimicked a little, try to be less conscious of what you're doing. Remember: This is something that humans (including you) do naturally, so at some point, it will begin to feel effortless. It's like driving a car. When you first learn, you have to be conscious and deliberate. But once you've acquired some experience, you can proceed by instinct.

Again, the objective here isn't to be false. It's to be strategic—by being human. "Subtle mimicry comes across as a form of flattery, the physical dance of charm itself," *The New York Times* has noted. "And if that kind of flattery doesn't close a deal, it may just be that the customer isn't buying."

Pull up a chair.

Jeff Bezos, the founder of Amazon.com, has accomplished a great deal in his forty-eight years. He's reshaped the retail business. He's become one of the thirty wealthiest people on the planet. And with far less fanfare, he's devised one of the best attunement practices I've encountered.

Amazon, like most organizations, has lots of meetings. But at the important ones, alongside the chairs in which his executives, marketing mavens, and software jockeys take their places, Bezos includes one more chair that remains empty. It's there to remind those assembled who's really the most important person in the room: the customer.

The empty chair has become legendary in Amazon's Seattle headquarters. Seeing it encourages meeting attendees to take the perspective of that invisible but essential person. What's going through her mind? What are her desires and concerns? What would she think of the ideas we're putting forward?

Try this in your own world. If you're crafting a presentation, the empty chair can represent the audience and its interests. If you're gathering material for a sales call, it can help generate possible objections and questions the other party might raise. If you're preparing a lesson plan, an empty chair can remind you to see things from your students' perspective.

Attuning yourself to others—exiting your own perspective and entering theirs—is essential to moving others. One smart, easy, and effective way to get inside people's heads is to climb into their chairs.

Get in touch with your inner ambivert.

Wharton's Adam Grant has discovered that the most effective salespeople are ambiverts, those who fall somewhere in the middle of the introversion-extraversion scale.

Are you one of them?

Take a moment to find out. Visit this link—http://www .danpink.com/assessment—where I've replicated the assessment that social scientists use to measure introversion and extraversion. It will take about five minutes to complete and you'll get a rating when you're done.

If you find you're an ambivert, congrats on being average! Continue what you're doing.

If you test as an extravert, try practicing some of the skills of an introvert. For example, make fewer declarations and ask more questions. When you feel the urge to assert, hold back instead. Most of all, talk less and listen more.

If you turn out to be an introvert, work on some of the skills of an extravert. Practice your "ask" in advance, so you don't flinch from it when the moment arrives. Goofy as it might sound, make a conscious effort to smile and sit up straight. Even if it's uncomfortable, speak up and state your point of view.

Most of us aren't on the extremes—uniformly extraverted or rigidly introverted. We're in the middle—and that allows us to move up and down the curve, attuning ourselves as circumstances demand, and discovering the hidden powers of ambiversion.

Have a conversation with a time traveler.

Cathy Salit, whom you'll meet in Chapter 8, has an exercise to build the improvisational muscles of her actors that can also work to hone anyone's powers of attunement. She calls it "Conversation with a Time Traveler." It doesn't require any props or equipment, just a little imagination and a lot of work.

Here's how it goes:

Gather a few people and ask them to think of items that somebody from three hundred years ago would not recognize. A traffic light, maybe. A carry-out pizza. An airport screening machine. Then divide into groups of two. Each pair selects an item. One person plays the role of someone from the early 1700s. The other has to explain the item.

This is more difficult than it sounds. That person from three hundred years ago has a perspective wildly different from our own. For instance, to explain, say, a Big Mac bought from a drive-through window requires understanding a variety of underlying concepts: owning an automobile, consuming what three hundred years ago was a preposterous amount of meat, trusting someone you've likely never met and will never see again, and so on.

"This exercise immediately challenges your assumptions about the understandability of your message," Salit says. "You are forced to care about the worldview of the other person." That's something we all should be doing a lot more of in the present.

Map it.

Walking a mile in another's shoes sometimes requires a map. Here are two new varieties that can provide a picture of where people are coming from and where they might be going.

1. Discussion Map

In your next meeting, cut through the clutter of comments with a map that can help reveal the group's social cartography. Draw a diagram of where each person in the meeting is sitting. When the session begins, note who speaks first by marking an X next to that person's name. Then each time someone speaks, add an X next to that name. If someone directs her comments to a particular person rather than to the whole group, draw a line from the speaker to the recipient. When the meeting is done you'll get a visual representation of who's talking the most, who's sitting out, and who's the target of people's criticisms or blandishments. You can even do this for those increasingly ubiquitous conference calls. (In fact, it's easier because nobody can see you!) On page 93 is an example, which shows that the person with the initials JW talked the most, that many of the comments were directed at AB, and that SL and KC barely participated.

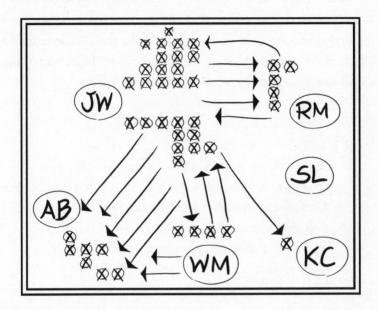

2. Mood Map

To gain a clear sense of a particular context, try mapping how it changes over time. For instance, in a meeting that involves moving others, note the mood at the beginning of the session. On a scale of 1 (negative and resistant) to 10 (positive and open), what's the temperature? Then, at what you think is the midpoint of the meeting, check the mood again. Has it improved? Deteriorated? Remained the same? Write down that number, too. Then do the same at the very end. Think of this as an emotional weather map to help you figure out whether conditions are brightening or growing stormier.

With attunement, you don't have to be a weatherman to know which way the wind blows.

Play "Mirror, mirror."

How attuned are you to slight alterations in appearances or situations? This team exercise, a favorite of change management consultants, can help you answer those questions and begin to improve. Gather your group and tell them to do the following:

1. Find a partner and stand face-to-face with that person for thirty seconds.
2. Then turn around so that you're both back-to-back with your partner.
3. Once turned around, each person changes one aspect of his or her appearance—for example, remove earrings, add eyeglasses, untuck your shirt. (Important: Don't tell people what you're going to ask them to do until they're back-to-back.) Wait sixty seconds.
4. Turn back around and see if you or your partner can tell what has changed.
5. Repeat this twice more with the same person, each time altering something new about your appearance.

When you're done, debrief with a short discussion. Which changes did people notice? Which eluded detection? How much of doing this well depended on being observant and attuned from the outset? How might this experience change your next encounter with a colleague, client, or student?

Find uncommon commonalities.

The research of Arizona State University social psychologist Robert Cialdini, some of which I'll discuss in Chapter 6, shows that we're more likely to be persuaded by those whom we like. And one reason we like people is that they remind us of . . . us.

Finding similarities can help you attune yourself to others and help them attune themselves to you. Here's an exercise that works well in teams and yields some insights individuals can later deploy on their own.

Assemble a group of three or four people and pose this question: What do we have in common, either with another person or with everyone? Go beyond the surface. For example, does everybody have a younger brother? Have most people visited a Disney property in the last year? Are some people soccer fanatics or opera buffs or amateur cheese makers?

Set a timer for five minutes and see how many commonalities you can come up with. You might be surprised. Searching for similarities—Hey, I've got a dachshund, too!—may seem trivial. We dismiss such things as "small talk." But that's a mistake. Similarity—the genuine, not the manufactured, variety—is a key form of human connection. People are more likely to move together when they share common ground.

5.

Buoyancy

On Wednesday morning, the day after he'd sold about $150 worth of carpet sweepers and cleaning products to two San Francisco lawyers, Fuller Brush Man Norman Hall returns to their office to deliver the goods. But when he arrives, the lawyers have not. So Hall and I retreat to a break room situated in the corner of the building's seventh floor. The room is the aggressively generic sort of space you find in many office buildings—a small kitchen setup against one wall, a cheap table surrounded by cheaper chairs in the room's center. But it gives us a place to park. And there we sit, chatting about Hall's life, waiting for his customers to show up so he can give them their loot and get on with his day.

About a half-hour into our conversation, a woman who works down the hall enters the break room and begins preparing a small pot of coffee. When her back is turned, Hall signals with a raised index finger that he wants to interrupt our conversation to begin one with her.

"Are you the new office down the way?" he asks.

"We are," she says, turning her head, but not her body, to respond.

"I've been calling on these two attorneys here for many, many years. And I was going to introduce myself," Hall says. "I don't know whether there's much interest. But I've been covering this area of the city for almost forty years."

The woman, her back still turned and her voice devoid of even a fleck of emotion, says, "Uh-huh."

"I'm sure you've heard of Fuller Brush," Hall begins.

"Yeah . . . we . . . uh," she replies. She's uncomfortable. And it's clear that the encounter has become a game of beat the clock. Will her coffee finish brewing before Hall gets fully into his sales pitch? "I don't think we have any need."

Drip . . . drip . . . drip.

"I don't press myself on people," Hall assures her, calm in his voice and time on his side.

Drip . . . drip . . . drip.

"*Okaaay,*" she says, in the singsongy rising intonation of someone trying to end a conversation. "*Thaaank yoooou . . .*"

Hall pretends to be oblivious. "I carry the home catalog. And then I do supply certain offices with minor cleaning items. That's why I'm here," he says.

She turns, crosses her arms, and alternates her gaze between Hall and the coffee. Hall explains that the lawyers have been his customers for fifteen years and that he's waiting to give them what they ordered the day before. He tells her again that he's been working this neighborhood for four decades. He reiterates that he doesn't press, that he's not one of those pushy salesmen, that he simply has some products that might be useful, and that he can tell her about them in just a few minutes and not waste any of her time.

Drip . . . drip . . . the coffee is done.

"*Wellll*," the woman says, stretching the word for long enough that an outright no becomes a grudging maybe, "stop by on your way out."

Hall asks her name. It's Beth. She exits with her fresh cup of coffee. Silence fills the room. Hall waits until Beth is out of earshot. Then he leans in toward me across the break room table.

"That," he says, "is how it starts."

Norman Hall began selling Fuller brushes because he was broke. Born in New York City, the son of a Russian mother who took care of the household and a Scottish father who was a sales representative for a publishing company, Hall worked some as a child actor. But upon graduating from high school, he enrolled at Cornell University intent on becoming a doctor. "It quickly became apparent that medicine wasn't my best vocation," he told me. "I spent more time performing than studying."

After a stint in the U.S. Navy, he returned to New York City to give professional acting a serious try. It was difficult. In need of steady income, he followed his father's path and became a salesman for a publishing company. Before long, he found himself in San Francisco, opening the West Coast office of Grove Press, the imprint that published Jack Kerouac, William Burroughs, and Allen Ginsberg. In a few years, that office cratered. So did Hall's marriage. He started a restaurant, which flopped and burned through his savings.

It was the early 1970s, and "I was down to my last buck," Hall said. "I answered an ad for Fuller Brushes because it offered very fast turnover and quick cash flow."

He quit four times the first week.

Although he'd been a salesperson before, and therefore had

met with his full share of rejection, he found door-to-door selling especially brutal. These rejections came fast and ferociously, often in the form of a rude comment and a slammed door. But every time he wanted to quit, one of the San Francisco office's veteran salesmen pulled him aside. This fellow—Charlie was his name—was "the quintessential Fuller Brush man," Hall said. He encouraged Hall, telling him that the nos he was piling up were just part of the process, and that he should "keep going, keep going."

"By God, at the end of the week, I had a nice wage for myself," Hall said.

Hall did keep going, still trying his hand at acting and looking for other ways to support himself. "It was a day-to-day thing," he said. "But after about five years, I finally reconciled to the fact that this is my career and I'd just do a damn good job of it."

Not that it's ever easy. But what wears him down isn't lugging boxes of hairbrushes and bottles of stain remover up and down roller-coastery hills or trekking five miles a day on seventy-five-year-old legs. It's something deeper. Each day, when he makes his rounds, Hall confronts what he calls "an ocean of rejection."

Draw a map of the world of selling and the most prominent topographical feature is that deep and menacing ocean. Anyone who sells—whether they're trying to convince customers to make a purchase or colleagues to make a change—must contend with wave after wave of rebuffs, refusals, and repudiations.

How to stay afloat amid that ocean of rejection is the second essential quality in moving others. I call this quality "buoyancy." Hall exemplifies it. Recent social science explains it. And if you understand buoyancy's three components—which apply before, during, and after any effort to move others—you can use it effectively in your own life.

Before: Interrogative Self-Talk

The hardest part of selling, Norman Hall says, occurs before his well-polished shoes even touch the streets of San Francisco. "Just getting myself out of the house and facing people" is the stiffest challenge, he says. "It's that big, unknown faceless person I have to face for the first time."

Most sales and success gurus offer a standard remedy for Hall's hesitation: He should pump himself up. He should take a moment to remind himself how fabulous and unstoppable he is. For example, Og Mandino, whose inspirational books helped set the tone for sales advice in the twentieth century, recommended that we each should tell ourselves, "I am nature's greatest miracle" and that "I will be the greatest salesman the world has ever known."[1] Napoleon Hill—author of *Think and Grow Rich*, one of the best-selling American books of the last century—wrote that the "first step in salesmanship" was "autosuggestion," "the principle through which the salesman saturates his own mind with belief in the commodity or service offered for sale, as well as in his own *ability* to sell."[2] From Anthony Robbins in the United States to Paul McKenna in the United Kingdom to any sales training course anywhere in the world, the advice arrives with remarkable sameness: Tell yourself you can do it. Declaring an unshakable belief in your inherent awesomeness inflates a sturdy raft that can keep you bobbing in an ocean of rejection.

Alas, the social science shows something different and more nuanced.

We human beings talk to ourselves all the time—so much, in fact, that it's possible to categorize our self-talk. Some of it is positive, as in "I'm strong," "I've got this," or "I will be the world's greatest salesman." Some of it—for a few of us, much of it—is negative. "I'm too weak to finish this race" or "I've never been good at math" or "There's no way I can sell these encyclopedias." But whether the talk is chest-thumping or ego-bashing, it tends to be declarative. It states what is or what will be.

However, the person whose example you should be following takes a different tack. His name is Bob the Builder. And if you haven't been around preschool children in the last fifteen years, let me offer a quick dossier. Bob is an overall-clad, hard-hat-sporting, stop-motion-animated guy who runs a construction company. His TV program, which began in England in 1999, now entertains kids in forty-five countries. Bob is always finding himself in sticky situations that seem inevitably to call for traditional sales or non-sales selling. Like all of us, Bob talks to himself. But Bob's self-talk is neither positive nor declarative. Instead, to move himself and his team, he asks a question: *Can we fix it?*

Devotees of Mandino, Hill, Robbins, and McKenna might shudder at allowing this shaft of doubt—questioning one's ability?—to shine through our psychic windows. But social scientists are discovering that Bob has it right. Yes, positive self-talk is generally more effective than negative self-talk. But the most effective self-talk of all doesn't merely shift emotions. It shifts linguistic *categories*. It moves from making statements to asking questions.

Three researchers—Ibrahim Senay and Dolores Albarracín of the University of Illinois, along with Kenji Noguchi of the University of Southern Mississippi—confirmed the efficacy of "interrogative self-talk" in a series of experiments they conducted in 2010. In one, they gave participants ten anagrams to solve (for example, rearranging the letters in "when" to spell "hewn"). They separated the participants into two groups, each of which was treated identically except for the one minute before they tackled their assignments. The researchers instructed the first group to *ask* themselves whether they would solve the puzzles—and the second group to *tell* themselves that they would solve the puzzles. On average, the self-questioning group solved nearly 50 percent more puzzles than the self-affirming group.[3]

In the next experiment, the researchers presented a new group of participants with another round of anagrams, but they added a twist of trickery: "We told participants that we were interested in people's handwriting practices. With this pretense, participants were given a sheet of paper to write down 20 times one of the following words: *Will I, I will, I,* or *Will.*"[4]

The outcome was similar. People who'd written *Will I* solved nearly twice as many anagrams as those who'd written *I will, Will,* or *I.* In subsequent experiments, the basic pattern held. Those who approached a task with Bob-the-Builder-style questioning self-talk outperformed those who employed the more conventional juice-myself-up declarative self-talk.

The reasons are twofold. First, the interrogative, by its very form, elicits answers—and within those answers are strategies for actually carrying out the task. Imagine, for instance, that you're readying yourself for an important meeting in which you must pitch an idea and marshal support for it. You could tell yourself, "I'm the best. This is going to be a breeze," and that might give you a short-term emotional boost. But if you instead ask, "Can I make a great pitch?" the research has found that you provide yourself something that reaches deeper and lasts longer. You might respond to yourself, "Well, yes, I can make a great pitch. In fact, I've probably pitched ideas at meetings two dozen times in my life." You might remind yourself of your preparation. "Sure, I can do this. I know this material inside out and I've got some great examples to persuade the people who might be skeptical." You might also give yourself specific tactical advice. "At the last meeting like this, I spoke too quickly—so this time I'll slow down. Sometimes in these situations, I get flustered by questions, so this time I'll take a breath before responding." Mere affirmation feels good and that helps. But it doesn't prompt you to summon the resources and strategies to actually accomplish the task.

The second reason is related. Interrogative self-talk, the researchers say, "may inspire thoughts about autonomous or intrinsically motivated reasons to pursue a goal."[5] As ample research has demonstrated, people are more likely to act, and to perform well, when the motivations come from intrinsic choices rather than from extrinsic pressures.[6] Declarative self-talk risks bypassing one's motivations. Questioning self-talk elicits the reasons for doing something and reminds people that many of those reasons come from within.[*]

To help get us out of the door, then, the first component in buoyancy is interrogative self-talk.

Can you do that?

Well, you'll have to ask yourself.

During: Positivity Ratios

I'm pretty sure Norman Hall is an ambivert. A few days in his company proves he's not a hard-core introvert. Besides, he couldn't have earned a living selling brushes for forty years if he were skittish about speaking up or uncomfortable around strangers. But

---

[*]We'll see a similar phenomenon at work in the "question pitch" in Chapter 7.

Hall isn't exactly a wrist-grabbing, backslapping extravert either. He's thoughtful, deliberate, and—as he often describes himself—soft-spoken.

"I hate salesmen who are used-car types, who press and press and press. And I don't want to be one of those guys," he told me. "I am more soft-spoken in my work than I am in my real life." Like all effective sellers, Hall is a master of attunement. He listens and observes more than the stereotypical yap-yapping salesman, but he also adds his voice and makes his case with vigor when the situation demands. And if you watch his ambiversion in action and listen carefully to what he says and how he interacts with others, he also demonstrates the second component of buoyancy: positivity.

"Positivity" is one of those words that make many of us roll our eyes, gather our belongings, and look for the nearest exit. It has the saccharine scent of the pumped-up and dumbed-down, an empty concept pushed by emptier people. But a host of recent research testifies to its importance in many realms of life, including how we move others.

Consider, for instance, a difficult negotiation in which each side is trying to sell the other on its position. The conventional view holds that negotiators shouldn't necessarily be nasty and brutish but that they should remain tough-minded and poker-faced.

A few years ago, a team of behavioral scientists led by Shirli Kopelman of the University of Michigan tested this proposition by simulating a series of negotiations. In one experiment, they presented their participants, executives who were pursuing MBAs, with the following scenario. You're planning a wedding. Several weeks ago, you made provisional arrangements with a catering company that had provided a good-faith estimate of $14,000 for its services. Now you are about to meet the caterer's business manager, who's come bearing bad news. Because of market fluctuations, the estimate has increased to $16,995. What's more, the caterer has another client ready to take the date if you don't sign the contract.

Unbeknownst to the participants, they'd been divided into three groups. And while the "business manager" (a specially trained actor) gave each of the three groups precisely the same explanation for the changed price, and offered identical terms and conditions for the catering, she varied her emotional approach. To one group, she displayed positive emotions. She "spoke with a friendly tone, smiled often, nodded her head in agreement, and appeared cordial and inviting." To another, she "spoke antagonistically, appeared intimidating, and was insistent." To the final group, she "used an even and monotonic voice, displayed little emotion, and spoke in a pragmatic manner."[7]

The business manager's affect had a significant effect. Those who'd heard the positive-inflected pitch were twice as likely to accept the deal as those who'd heard the negative one—even though the terms were identical. In a subsequent similar experiment, in which negotiators were able to make counteroffers, those who'd dealt with the negative person made far less generous counteroffers than those dealing with someone positive on the other side of the table.[8]

Barbara Fredrickson of the University of North Carolina is the leading researcher on positivity—her catchall term for a basket of emotions including amusement, appreciation, joy, interest, gratitude, and inspiration. Negative emotions, she says, evolved to narrow people's vision and propel their behavior toward survival in the moment (*I'm frightened, so I'll flee. I'm angry, so I'll fight*). By contrast, "Positive emotions do the opposite: They *broaden* people's ideas about possible actions, opening our awareness to a wider range of thoughts and . . . making us more receptive and more creative," she writes.[9]

The broadening effect of positive emotions has important consequences for moving others. Consider both sides of a typical transaction. For the seller, positive emotions can widen her view of her counterpart and his situation. Where negative emotions help us see trees, positive ones reveal forests. And that, in turn, can aid in devising unexpected solutions to the buyer's problem. Other studies show that positive emotions can expand our behavioral repertoires and heighten intuition and creativity,[10] all of which enhance our effectiveness. What's more, as we saw in Kopelman's study, emotions can be contagious. That is, the effects of positivity during a sales encounter infect the buyer, making him less adversarial, more open to possibility, and perhaps willing to reach an agreement in which both parties benefit. And when both sides leave the table satisfied, that can establish a sustained relationship and smooth the way for subsequent transactions.

Positivity has one other important dimension when it comes to moving others. "You have to believe in the product you're selling— and that has to show," Hall says. Nearly every salesperson I talked to disputed the idea that some people "could sell anything"— whether they believed in it or not. That may have been true in the past, when sellers held a distinct information advantage and buyers had limited choices. But today, these salespeople told me, believing leads to a deeper understanding of your offering, which allows sellers to better match what they have with what others need. And genuine conviction can also produce emotional contagion of its own. For instance, Cory Scherer and Brad Sagarin of Northern Illinois University have found that inserting a mild profanity like "damn" into a speech increases the persuasiveness of the speech and listeners' perception of the speaker's intensity.[11] "I believe in these products," Hall told me. "I know damn well that when you buy one of these brushes you're going to have it for years."

But fear not, those of you who prefer to salt your life's stew with several shakes of negativity. Remember: Interrogative self-talk is the smart choice when *preparing* to move someone. And positivity during your efforts doesn't mean coating yourself or others in a thick glaze of sugar. In fact, a particular recipe—a golden ratio of positivity—leads to the best results.

In research she carried out with Marcial Losada, a Brazilian social scientist who uses mathematical models and complexity theory to analyze team behavior,[12] Fredrickson had a group of participants record their positive and negative emotions each day for four weeks.* She and Losada calculated the ratio of positive to negative emotions of the participants—and then compared these ratios with the participants' scores on a thirty-three-item measurement of their overall well-being.

What they found is that those with an equal—that is, 1 to 1 —balance of positive and negative emotions had no higher well-being than those whose emotions were predominantly negative. Both groups generally were languishing. Even more surprising, people whose ratio was 2 to 1 positive-to-negative were also no happier than those whose negative emotions exceeded their positive ones. But once the balance between emotions hit a certain number, everything tipped. That number was 2.9013, which, for the sake of readers who don't need the precision of the fourth decimal place, Fredrickson and Losada round up to 3. Once positive emotions outnumbered negative emotions by 3 to 1—that is, for every three instances of feeling gratitude, interest, or contentment, they experi-

---

*"Positive emotions included amusement, awe, compassion, contentment, gratitude, hope, interest, joy, love, pride, and sexual desire. Negative emotions included anger, contempt, disgust, embarrassment, fear, guilt, sadness, and shame," the researchers explain.

enced only one instance of anger, guilt, or embarrassment—people generally flourished. Those below that ratio usually did not.[13] But Fredrickson and Losada also found that positivity had an upper limit. Too much can be as unproductive as too little. Once the ratio hit about 11 to 1, positive emotions began doing more harm than good. Beyond that balance of positive-to-negative, life becomes a festival of Panglossian cluelessness, where self-delusion suffocates self-improvement. Some negativity—what Fredrickson and Losada call "appropriate negativity"—is essential. Without it, "behavior patterns calcify."[14] Negative emotions offer us feedback on our performance, information on what's working and what's not, and hints about how to do better.

Hall seems to have found the proper mix. He says that he tries to begin his day with one or two sales calls that he knows will be friendly. He also seeks positive interactions throughout his day. For instance, in one three-hour stretch I was with him, he visited a restaurant to ask after a friend who worked there who'd been ill. He stopped a longtime customer on the street to catch up on what was going on in his life. He entered a clothing store, was greeted by its proprietor with a hearty "Mr. Fuller!" and the two embraced, albeit in an awkward bro hug. These experiences help him "keep going, keep going" after other visits, where he leaves muttering under his breath at people's rudeness.

Fredrickson sees the healthy positivity ratios of Hall and others as a calibration between two competing pulls: levity and gravity. "Levity is that unseen force that lifts you skyward, whereas gravity is the opposing force that pulls you earthward. Unchecked levity leaves you flighty, ungrounded, and unreal. Unchecked gravity leaves you collapsed in a heap of misery," she writes. "Yet when properly combined, these two opposing forces leave you buoyant."[15]

After: Explanatory Style

At the end of each day, Norman Hall boards a Golden Gate Transit bus and rides back home to his wife in Rohnert Park, about ninety minutes away. Some days he reads. Other times he sleeps. Many afternoons he just thinks. But how he thinks about his day—in particular how he explains its worst aspects—can go a long way in determining whether he succeeds. This is the third component in buoyancy.

One of the towering figures in contemporary psychological science is Martin Seligman, the University of Pennsylvania scholar who helped originate "positive psychology," which treats happiness, well-being, and satisfaction with the same intensity and analytic rigor with which the field has long treated dysfunction, debility, and despair. One of Seligman's signal contributions has been to deepen our understanding of optimism.

Seligman arrived at the topic from the other end of the emotional tunnel. As a young scientist in the 1970s, he'd pioneered the concept of "learned helplessness." First with studies on dogs, and later with research on humans, Seligman pushed back against the prevailing behavioralist view, which held that all creatures, whether they walked on two legs or four, responded systematically and predictably to external rewards and punishments. Seligman's work demonstrated that after extended experiences in which they were stripped of any control over their environment, some individuals just gave up. Even when conditions returned to normal, and they once again possessed the ability to seek gain or avoid pain, they didn't act. They had learned to be helpless.

In human beings, Seligman observed, learned helplessness was usually a function of people's "explanatory style"—their habit of explaining negative events to themselves. Think of explanatory style as a form of self-talk that occurs after (rather than before) an experience. People who give up easily, who become helpless even in situations where they actually can do something, explain bad events as *permanent*, *pervasive*, and *personal*. They believe that negative conditions will endure a long time, that the causes are universal rather than specific to the circumstances, and that they're the ones to blame. So if their boss yells at them, they interpret it as "My boss is always mean" or "All bosses are jerks" or "I'm incompetent at my job" rather than "My boss is having an awful day and I just happened to be in the line of fire when he lost it." A pessimistic explanatory style—the habit of believing that "it's my fault, it's going to last forever, and it's going to undermine everything I do"[16]—is debilitating, Seligman found. It can diminish performance, trigger depression, and "turn setbacks into disasters."[17]

By the mid-1980s, after learned helplessness had become a staple of introductory psychology courses, Seligman and some colleagues began wondering whether the theory had a sunnier flip side. If people with a downbeat explanatory style suffered, do people with an upbeat style thrive? To find out, Seligman and his University of Pennsylvania colleague Peter Schulman sought a territory awash in disappointment, one whose inhabitants every day faced wave after wave of negative reactions: sales.

The two researchers assembled nearly one hundred sales agents from the Pennsylvania region of the Metropolitan Life Insurance Company. These men (and a few women) held classic sales jobs. They made cold calls to set up appointments, met with prospects to pitch policies, and earned their living from commissions on the sales they closed. Seligman and Schulman gave all the agents the Attributional Style Questionnaire (ASQ), a psychological assessment that offers a series of vignettes, the responses to which locate the person's explanatory style on a pessimism-optimism spectrum. Then they tracked the agents' performance over the next two years, measuring how much insurance they sold and the total commissions they earned.

The results were unequivocal. "Agents who scored in the optimistic half of explanatory style sold 37% more insurance than agents scoring in the pessimistic half. Agents in the top decile sold 88% more insurance than those in the bottom decile," they discovered.[18]

Next, in response to Metropolitan Life's concern that about half of its sales agents quit their jobs in the first year, Seligman and Schulman studied a different group—more than one hundred newly hired salespeople. Before these agents started their jobs, the researchers gave them the ASQ. Then they charted their progress. Agents who scored in the pessimistic half of the ASQ ended up quitting at twice the rate of those in the optimistic half. Agents in the most pessimistic quarter were three times as likely to quit as those in the most optimistic 25 percent.[19]

In other words, the salespeople with an optimistic explanatory style—who saw rejections as temporary rather than permanent, specific rather than universal, and external rather than personal— sold more insurance and survived in their jobs much longer. What's more, explanatory style predicted performance with about the same accuracy as the most widely used insurance industry assessment for hiring agents. Optimism, it turns out, isn't a hollow sentiment. It's a catalyst that can stir persistence, steady us during challenges, and stoke the confidence that we can influence our surroundings.

Norman Hall has the optimistic explanatory style down. When he was rejected, as he was several times during the sales calls on which I joined him, he explained the rejections as temporary, specific, or external. The jewelry store owner was busy with a customer and couldn't focus on brushes. The maintenance guy hadn't carefully assessed his supplies yet. The clothing store manager was probably having cash-flow problems in a tight economy. When I asked him about these rebuffs, Hall was unperturbed. "I'm a damn good salesman," he told me. "You have to keep going. That's it."

Still, the glasses Hall wears have clear lenses—not rose-colored ones. He finds some customers annoying. He admits to taking some rejections personally. He's had plenty of grim, unpleasant days. But negative events can clarify positive ones. They equip Hall not with weak-kneed dreaminess but with tough-minded buoyancy—the proper balance between downward and upward forces. His is not blind optimism but what Seligman calls "flexible optimism—optimism with its eyes open."[20]

The first thing we hear is panting. That's followed by the *clumpety-clump* of four feet on the hallway carpet. Penelope Chronis and Liz Kreher, their dog in tow, are arriving to open their office and begin their day. They are surprised to see Norman Hall—they'd placed their order less than twenty-four hours ago—but are delighted to get their electrostatic carpet sweeper and stainless-steel scrubbers. It also turns out that they know Beth, the woman from the break room, and encourage Hall to use their names as a way for him to gain credibility.

His delivery made, Hall and I walk down the corridor toward Beth's office. At this point, I feel like my presence is cramping Hall's style. He doesn't need a wingman on this sales call, so when he enters her lobby, I head for the elevators.

It's about 11:00 A.M. when we split paths, and I wait for Hall on the sidewalk in front of 530 Bush Street. Beth had shown barely a crease of interest in brushes or much else back in the break room, so I expect Hall to be down by 11:05. He's not.

Nor is he down at 11:10. Or 11:15. Or 11:20.

It's not until nearly 11:25 that Hall pushes through the glass doors on the ground level of the office building and walks toward the sidewalk.

I look at him but don't say a word. I just open my palms upward and raise my eyebrows to ask, "Well?"

He shakes his head and, with the forefinger of his right hand extended parallel to the ground, he makes a slashing motion across this throat.

No sale.

We walk in silence for maybe eight steps. Then the last Fuller Brush Man in San Francisco turns to me and says, "But I think there's going to be a chance to get her next time."

SAMPLE CASE

Buoyancy

Be like Bob: Practice interrogative self-talk.

Next time you're getting ready to persuade others, reconsider how you prepare. Instead of pumping yourself up with declarations and affirmations, take a page from Bob the Builder and pose a question instead.

Ask yourself: "Can I move these people?"

As social scientists have discovered, interrogative self-talk is often more valuable than the declarative kind. But don't simply leave the question hanging in the air like a lost balloon. Answer it—directly and in writing. List five specific reasons why the answer to your question is yes. These reasons will remind you of the strategies that you'll need to be effective on the task, providing a sturdier and more substantive grounding than mere affirmation.

In other words, ask and you shall receive.

Monitor your positivity ratio.

It's the golden mean of well-being, the magic formula for flourishing, the secret numerical code of the satisfied: 3 to 1. What can you do to ensure your balance between positive and negative emotions reaches that elusive ratio?

One way to begin is to visit Barbara Fredrickson's website (http://positivityratio.com/). Take her "Positivity Self Test"—a twenty-question assessment you can complete in two or three minutes that will yield your current positivity ratio. Then establish a free account and track your ratio over time. (You can find background on the test in Fredrickson's book, *Positivity: Top-Notch Research Reveals the 3 to 1 Ratio That Will Change Your Life*, an excellent popular introduction to her academic work.)

In addition, be more conscious of your emotions in the moment. In fact, try listing Fredrickson's ten positive emotions—joy, gratitude, serenity, interest, hope, pride, amusement, inspiration, awe, and love—on your phone, computer, or office wall. Select one or two. Then in the course of the day, look for ways to display those emotions. This will give you a psychic boost, lift up the people around you, and increase your chances of moving others. Am I sure? I'm positive.

Tweak your explanatory style.

Martin Seligman's work has demonstrated that how we explain negative events has an enormous effect on our buoyancy and ultimately our performance. Start revamping your explanatory style in ways science has shown are effective.

When something bad occurs, ask yourself three questions—and come up with an intelligent way to answer each one "no":

1. **Is this permanent?**

   Bad response: "Yes. I've completely lost my skill for moving others."

   Better response: "No. I was flat today because I haven't been getting enough sleep."

2. **Is this pervasive?**

   Bad response: "Yes. Everyone in this industry is impossible to deal with."

   Better response: "No. This particular guy was a jerk."

3. **Is this personal?**

   Bad response: "Yes. The reason he didn't buy is that I messed up my presentation."

   Better response: "No. My presentation could have been better, but the real reason he passed is that he wasn't ready to buy right now."

The more you explain bad events as *temporary, specific,* and *external*, the more likely you are to persist even in the face of adversity.

As some positive psychologists have put it, the key is to "dispute" and "de-catastrophize" negative explanations. To dispute, confront each explanation the way a sharp lawyer would cross-examine a witness. Poke holes in its story. Question its premises. Identify internal contradictions. To de-catastrophize, ask yourself: What are the overall consequences and why are those consequences not nearly as calamitous as they seem on the surface?

For more information, visit Seligman's website (http://www
.authentichappiness.sas.upenn.edu/Default.aspx), and take his Optimism Test to get a sense of your current style. And check out
his classic book, *Learned Optimism: How to Change Your Mind and
Your Life.*

Try the "enumerate and embrace" strategy.

One way to remain buoyant is to acquire a more realistic sense
of what can actually sink you. You can do that by counting your
rejections—and then celebrating them. It's a strategy I call "enu-
merate and embrace."

1. Enumerate.

Try actually counting the nos you get during a week. Use one of the
many free counter apps available for smartphones and tally every
time your efforts to move others meet with resistance. (You analog
types can use a small notebook and pen, which work just as well.)

By the end of the week, you might be surprised by just how
many nos the world has delivered to your doorstep. However, you
might be more surprised by something else: You're still around.
Even in that weeklong ocean of rejection, you've still managed to
stay afloat. That realization can give you the will to continue and
the confidence to do even better the following week.

2. Embrace.

For the really big Nos, consider following the lead of Jay Goldberg,
founder of the Bergino Baseball Clubhouse, an art gallery and

memorabilia store in New York City. Early in his career, Goldberg was working for a prominent American political consultant, but what he really wanted was a job in Major League Baseball. So he sent letters to all twenty-six MLB teams asking for an interview, an internship, anything that would give him a chance. Twenty-five of the teams sent him rejection letters. (The New York Yankees never responded.)

Goldberg kept those letters. And when he launched his own sports agency in the early 1990s, he framed each one and hung all twenty-five on his office wall. "It was my way of showing that I didn't quit," he says. "I got all these rejections, but kept going." Even better, representatives of some of the teams that rejected him found themselves gazing at their earlier decision when they negotiated with Goldberg over one of his clients. "The letters gave me a little smile every time I looked at them." These days, Goldberg has them in his office at his popular baseball retail space, reminding him daily that how you see rejection often depends on how you frame it.

Don't forget to go negative every once in a while.

Every silver lining has a cloud. Buoyancy, whether positivity ratios or explanatory style, isn't about banishing the negative. Negativity and negative emotions are crucial for our survival. They prevent unproductive behaviors from cementing into habits. They deliver useful information on our efforts. They alert us to when we're on the wrong path.

As Fredrickson explains, "Life gives us plenty of reasons to be afraid, angry, sad, and then some. Without negativity you . . . lose touch with reality. You're not genuine. In time, you drive people away." So allow yourself what she dubs "appropriate negativity"—moments of anger, hostility, disgust, and resentment that serve a productive purpose. For instance, suppose you fail to convince a client to sign on for another year. If part of the reason was that some of your work this year wasn't up to your typical standards, get a little angry with yourself. You screwed up this time. Then use that negative emotion as the impetus to improve.

And consider a few dollops of what Wellesley College's Julie Norem calls "defensive pessimism." Her work has shown that thinking through gloom-and-doom scenarios and mentally preparing for the very worst that can occur helps some people effectively manage their anxieties. If this approach sounds useful, present yourself with a series of "What ifs?" What if everything goes wrong? What if the unthinkable happens? What if this is the worst decision of my life? These questions could prompt answers you didn't expect, which might calm you down and even lift you up.

Send yourself a rejection letter.

Even in an age of text messages and Twitpics, rejection still often arrives in the form of a sheet of letterhead folded into a paper envelope. Nobody likes receiving rejection letters. But one way to reduce their sting, and perhaps even avoid one altogether, is to preempt the rejecter by writing the letter yourself.

Say you're interviewing for a new job or trying to raise money from an investor. Take an hour and write yourself a letter from the person you're trying to move explaining why his answer is "Thanks, but no thanks." List the reasons he's turning you down. And, of course, include the irritating phrases—"After careful consideration . . . ," "We regret to inform you . . . ," and "We had many qualified applicants . . . ," and so on—that are standard for this genre.

When you read your letter, you'll probably laugh. Once the rejection is in writing, its consequences can seem far less dire. More important, by articulating the reasons for turning you down, the letter might reveal soft spots in what you're presenting, which you can then work to strengthen.

And if you're too lazy to write the letter yourself, try out the Rejection Generator Project (http://ow.ly/cQ5rl). Just choose your favored style of repudiation, type in your e-mail address, and in minutes you'll receive a dream destroyer in your inbox. We regret to inform you that the site is designed for writers trying to sell manuscripts to publishers, but its results can apply to anyone, even you. We wish you well in your future endeavors.

6.

Clarity

Forgive the intrusion into your personal affairs, but let me ask: Are you saving enough for retirement? If you're like many people, your answer is a quiet and sheepish "Uh, probably not." Around the world, but especially in the United States, the number of individuals who haven't made adequate preparations for their golden years stands somewhere between grim and alarming. About half of U.S. households are financially unprepared for their breadwinners to retire at age sixty-five. Three in four Americans have less than $30,000 saved in their retirement accounts.[1]

It's not entirely our fault. Partly because our brains evolved at a time when the future itself was perilous, we human beings are notoriously bad at wrapping our minds around far-off events. Our biases point us toward the present. So when given a choice between an immediate reward (say, $1,000 right now) and a reward we have to wait for ($1,150 in two years), we'll often take the former even when it's in our own interest to choose the latter.

Policy makers and social scientists have devised a few methods to help us overcome our weakness. One technique, akin to Odysseus's strapping himself to the mast to sail past the Sirens, restricts our ability to choose. We ask our employer to automatically deduct a set amount from every paycheck and funnel it into our retirement account—which allows us to do the right thing by default rather than by taking affirmative steps. Another is to make our choices and consequences more concrete—for example, by reminding ourselves that the $1,150 we'll get in two years could be a down payment on a new car to replace our current auto, which probably won't last much beyond twenty-four months.[2]

But Hal Hershfield, a social psychologist at New York University, thought the barrier to moving people to save for retirement might be something else altogether. Working with six far-flung colleagues, he conducted a series of studies to test a different hypothesis. In one experiment, Hershfield and team had each of their participants strap on a virtual reality headset. Half the participants saw a digital representation of themselves—an avatar—for about a minute and then had a brief conversation with a digital representation of a researcher. The other half also saw an avatar of themselves through the headset. But for this group, researchers used a computer software package that ages faces to create an avatar that showed what the participant would look like at age seventy. This group gazed at the seventy-year-old version of themselves for about a minute and then had the same brief conversation with the researcher's avatar.

Afterward, the experimenters gave both groups a money allocation task. Imagine, they told the participants, that you've just received an unexpected $1,000. How would you allocate the money among the following four options?

- "Use it to buy something nice for someone special."
- "Invest it in a retirement fund."
- "Plan a fun and extravagant occasion."
- "Put it in a checking account."

Those who saw images of their current selves (call them the "Me Now" group) directed an average of $80 into the retirement account. Those who saw images of their future selves (the "Me Later" group) allocated more than twice that amount—$172.[3]

To determine more precisely what was driving the discrepancy in response—whether it was the sight of their own aging face or the reminder of aging in general—the researchers tried a similar experiment with a different set of participants. This time, half the participants saw an age-morphed image of themselves ("Me Later") and half saw an age-morphed image of someone else ("You Later"). The results weren't even close. Those who saw the image of themselves at age seventy saved more than those who'd simply seen a picture of a seventy-year-old. When researchers conducted similar experiments using equipment less complicated than an immersive virtual reality environment, the pattern held. The "Me Later" group always saved more.[4]

The problem we have saving for retirement, these studies showed, isn't only our meager ability to weigh present rewards against future ones. It is also the connection—or rather, the disconnection—between our present and future selves. Other research has shown that "thinking about the future self elicits neural activation patterns that are similar to neural activation patterns elicited by thinking about a stranger."[5] Envisioning ourselves far into the future is extremely difficult—so difficult, in fact, that we often think of that future self as an entirely different person. "To people estranged from their future selves, saving is like a choice between spending money today and giving it to a stranger years from now."[6]

Hershfield and his colleagues discovered that trying to solve an existing problem—getting people to better balance short-term and long-term rewards—was insufficient because it wasn't the problem that most needed solving. The researchers' breakthrough was to identify a new, and previously unknown, problem: that we think of ourselves today and ourselves in the future as different people. Once they identified that alternative problem, they were able to fashion a solution: Show people an image of themselves getting old. And that, in turn, addressed the broader concern—namely, encouraging people to save more money for retirement.

This conceptual shift demonstrates the third quality necessary in moving others today: clarity—the capacity to help others see their situations in fresh and more revealing ways and to identify problems they didn't realize they had.

Good salespeople, we've long been told, are skilled problem solvers. They can assess prospects' needs, analyze their predicaments, and deliver the optimal solutions. This ability to solve problems still matters. But today, when information is abundant and democratic rather than limited and privileged, it matters relatively less. After all, if I know precisely what my problem is—whether I'm hoping to buy a particular camera or I want to take a three-day beach vacation—I can often find the information I need to make my decision without any assistance. The services of others are far more valuable when I'm mistaken, confused, or completely clueless about my true problem. In those situations, the ability to move others hinges less on problem *solving* than on problem *finding*.

Finding the Right Problems to Solve

In the mid-1960s, two soon-to-be-legendary University of Chicago social scientists—Jacob Getzels and Mihaly Csikszentmihalyi—began studying the elusive subject of creativity. For one of his first investigations, in 1964, Csikszentmihalyi went to the nearby School of the Art Institute of Chicago and recruited about three dozen fourth-year art students for an experiment. He brought them into a studio that had two large tables. On one table were twenty-seven objects, exotic and mundane, that the school often used in its drawing classes. Csikszentmihalyi asked the students to select one or more objects from the first table, arrange a still life on the second table, and produce a drawing of the result. The young artists approached their task in two distinct ways. Some examined relatively few objects, outlined their idea swiftly, and moved quickly to draw their still life. Others took their time. They handled more objects, turned them this way and that, rearranged them several times, and needed much longer to complete the drawing. As Csikszentmihalyi saw it, the first group was trying to *solve* a problem: How can I produce a good drawing? The second was trying to *find* a problem: What good drawing can I produce?

Then Csikszentmihalyi conducted a mini art show of the student creations and asked a panel of art experts to evaluate the works. (These experts didn't know what Csikszentmihalyi was studying, nor did they know the source of the art.) When he tabulated the ratings, Csikszentmihalyi discovered that the experts deemed the problem finders' works far more creative than the problem solvers'. In 1970, Csikszentmihalyi and Getzels tracked down these same artists, now out of school and working for a living, to see how they were faring. About half the students had left the art world altogether. The other half was working, and often succeeding, as professional artists. The composition of that second group? Nearly all were problem finders back in their school days. When Csikszentmihalyi and Getzels followed up again in the early 1980s, they discovered that the problem finders "were 18 years later significantly more successful—by the standards of the artistic community—than their peers" who had approached their still-life drawings as more craftsmanlike problem solvers.[7] "The quality of the problem that is found is a forerunner of the quality of the solution that is attained . . ." Getzels concluded. "It is in fact the discovery and creation of problems rather than any superior knowledge, technical skill, or craftsmanship that often sets the creative person apart from others in his field."[8]

Although a few academics took issue with the Csikszentmihalyi–Getzels distinction between solving and finding,[9] the duo's research influenced both the modern understanding and the academic study of creativity. In subsequent research, they and other scholars found that people most disposed to creative breakthroughs in art, science, or any endeavor tend to be problem finders. These people sort through vast amounts of information and inputs, often from multiple disciplines; experiment with a variety of different approaches; are willing to switch directions in the course of a project; and often take longer than their counterparts to complete their work.

This more compelling view of the nature of problems has enormous implications for the new world of selling. Today, both sales and non-sales selling depend more on the creative, heuristic, problem-finding skills of artists than on the reductive, algorithmic, problem-solving skills of technicians. The reasons go back to the sea change described in Chapter 3. Only a short time ago, buyers faced several obstacles to solving problems on their own. So they relied on sellers, because sellers had access to information that the buyers did not. But today, the same move from information asymmetry to something approaching information equality that gave rise to the principle of *caveat venditor* is also reshaping what buyers can do for themselves and therefore what sellers must do to avoid irrelevance.

For instance, suppose I'm in the market for a new vacuum cleaner. Ten or fifteen years ago, I'd have had to go into a store, talk to a salesman who was much better informed than I ever could be, and then rely on him to provide the product I needed at a price that was fair. Today, I can solve the vacuum cleaner problem myself. I can go online and check out specs and ratings of various models. I can post a question on my Facebook page and seek recommendations from my friends and my "friends." Once I've settled on a few possibilities, I can compare prices with a few keystrokes. And I can order my choice from the vendor offering the best deal. I don't need a salesman at all.

Unless I've gotten my problem wrong.

After all, my ultimate aim isn't to acquire a vacuum cleaner. It's to have clean floors. Maybe my real problem is that the screens on my windows aren't sufficient to keep out dust, and replacing them with better screens will keep my entire house cleaner when the windows are open. Maybe my problem is that my carpet collects dirt too easily, and a new carpet will obviate the need for me to always be vacuuming. Maybe I shouldn't *buy* a vacuum cleaner but instead join a neighborhood cooperative that shares home appliances. Maybe there's an inexpensive cleaning service with its own equipment that serves my area. Someone who can help me achieve my main goal—clean floors—in a smarter, cheaper way is someone I'll listen to and perhaps even buy from. If I know my problem, I can likely solve it. If I don't know my problem, I might need some help finding it.

This theme eventually arises in almost any conversation about traditional sales. Take, for example, Ralph Chauvin, vice president of sales at Perfetti Van Melle, the Italian company that makes Mentos mints, AirHead fruit chews, and other delicacies. His sales force sells products to retailers who then stock their shelves and hope customers will buy. In the past few years he says he's seen a shift. Retailers are less interested in figuring out how many rolls of Mentos to order than in learning how to improve all facets of their operation. "They're looking for unbiased business partners," Chauvin told me. And that changes which salespeople are most highly prized. It isn't necessarily the "closers," those who can offer an immediate solution and secure the signature on the contract, he says. It's those "who can brainstorm with the retailers, who uncover new opportunities for them, and who realize that it doesn't matter if they close at that moment." Using a mix of number crunching and their own knowledge and expertise, the Perfetti salespeople tell retailers "what assortment of candy is the best for them to make the most money." That could mean offering five flavors of Mentos rather than seven. And it almost always means including products from competitors. In a sense, Chauvin says, his best salespeople think of their jobs not so much as selling candy but as selling insights about the confectionery business.

It's similar in other places and industries. In Tokyo, I sat down with Koji Takagi in a plush conference room across the street from the city's central Tokyo Station. Takagi is one of Japan's top sales gurus, president of the sales consultancy Celebrain and the author of several books. He told me that when he first started, having access to information and being able to wield it was what often determined sales success. Today, when information is ubiquitous, he said the premium is now on "the ability to hypothesize," to clarify what's going to happen next. Or take Shyam Sankar, the fellow from Chapter 2 who oversees Palantir Technologies' "forward-deployed engineers" who sell but who aren't salespeople. "The most important thing they do," he told me, "is find the right problems to solve."

This transformation from problem solving to problem finding as a central attribute in moving others reaches wide. For instance, the Haas School of Business at the University of California, Berkeley, now offers a course called "Problem Finding, Problem Solving" because, as its instructor says, "part of being an innovative leader is being able to frame a problem in interesting ways and . . . to see what the problem really is before you jump in to solve it." And a few years ago, the Conference Board, the well-regarded U.S. business group, gave 155 public school superintendents and eighty-nine private employers a list of cognitive capacities and asked their respondents to rate these capacities according to which are most important in today's workforce. The superintendents ranked "problem solving" number one. But the employers ranked it number eight. Their top-ranked ability: "problem identification."[10]

Identifying problems as a way to move others takes two longstanding skills and turns them upside down. First, in the past, the best salespeople were adept at *accessing* information. Today, they must be skilled at *curating* it—sorting through the massive troves of data and presenting to others the most relevant and clarifying pieces. Second, in the past, the best salespeople were skilled at *answering* questions (in part because they had information their prospects lacked). Today, they must be good at *asking* questions—uncovering possibilities, surfacing latent issues, and finding unexpected problems. And one question in particular sits at the top of the list.

Finding Your Frames

Rosser Reeves, an American advertising executive from the middle of the twentieth century, has three claims to fame. First, he coined the term "unique selling proposition," the idea that any product or service in the marketplace has to specify what differentiates it from its competitors. Second, he was among the first ad men to produce television spots for American presidential campaigns—including a 1952 ad for Dwight D. Eisenhower that included the singing refrain "I like Ike" (a forerunner of the rhyming pitch we'll discuss in Chapter 7). Third, Reeves is the protagonist in one of the most famous stories in advertising, one that exemplifies the enduring power of clarity.

The precise details of the story are somewhat in doubt. As it's been retold over the past fifty years, the particulars often change. But the broad contours of the tale go something like this:

One afternoon, Reeves and a colleague were having lunch in Central Park. On the way back to their Madison Avenue office, they encountered a man sitting in the park, begging for money. He had a cup for donations and beside it was a sign, handwritten on cardboard, that read: I AM BLIND.

Unfortunately for the man, the cup contained only a few coins. His attempts to move others to donate money were coming up short. Reeves thought he knew why. He told his colleague something to the effect of: "I bet I can dramatically increase the amount of money that guy is raising simply by adding four words to his sign." Reeves's skeptical friend took him up on the wager.

Reeves then introduced himself to the beleaguered man, explained that he knew something about advertising, and offered to change the sign ever so slightly to increase donations. The man agreed. Reeves took a marker and added his four words, and he and his friend stepped back to watch.

Almost immediately, a few people dropped coins into the man's cup. Other people soon stopped, talked to the man, and plucked dollar bills from their wallets. Before long, the cup was running over with cash, and the once sad-looking blind man, feeling his bounty, beamed.

What four words did Reeves add?

It is springtime and

The sign now read:

It is springtime and I am blind.

Reeves won his bet. And we learned a lesson. Clarity depends on contrast. In this case, the begging man's sign moved people in the park to empathize with him by starkly comparing their reality with his. Robert Cialdini, the Arizona State University scholar and one of the most important social scientists of the last generation, calls this "the contrast principle."[11] We often understand something better when we see it in comparison with something else than when we see it in isolation. In his work over the past three decades, Cialdini has recast how both academics and practitioners understand the dynamics of influencing others. And one of his core insights is that contrast operates within, and often amplifies, every aspect of persuasion.

That's why the most essential question you can ask is this: *Compared to what?*

You can raise that question by framing your offering in ways that contrast with its alternatives and therefore clarify its virtues.

The academic literature on framing is vast and sometimes conflicting.[12] But the following five frames can be useful in providing clarity to those you hope to move.

The less frame

Everybody loves choices. Yet ample research has shown that too much of a good thing can mutate into a bad thing. In one well-known study, Sheena Iyengar of Columbia University and Mark Lepper of Stanford set up booths at an upscale grocery store in Menlo Park, California, and offered shoppers the chance to taste and subsequently purchase different flavors of jam. The first booth offered twenty-four varieties. A week later, Iyengar and Lepper set up another booth with only six varieties. Not surprisingly, more customers stopped at the booth with the vast selection than at the one with fewer choices.

But when researchers examined what customers actually purchased, the results were so "striking" that "they appear[ed] to challenge a fundamental assumption underlying classic psychological theories of human motivation and economic theories of rational choice." Of the consumers who visited the booth with twenty-four varieties, only 3 percent bought jam. At the booth with a more limited selection, 30 percent made a purchase.[13] In other words, reducing consumers' options from twenty-four choices to six resulted in a tenfold increase in sales.

Or take a more recent study. This one asked participants to imagine they wanted to learn German. Then the researchers divided people into two groups. One group had to choose between a $575 online German-language course and a $449 German-language software package. The other group had to choose between that same $575 online course and the $449 software package *plus* a

German dictionary. Forty-nine percent of people in the first group picked the software package over the online course. But only 36 percent of the second group made that selection—despite its being a better deal. "Adding an inexpensive item to a product offering can lead to a decline in consumers' willingness to pay," the researchers concluded.[14] In many instances, addition can subtract.

This is why curation is so important, especially in a world saturated with options and alternatives. Framing people's options in a way that restricts their choices can help them see those choices more clearly instead of overwhelming them. What Mies van der Rohe said of designing buildings is equally true of moving those who inhabit them: Less is more.

The experience frame

Economists categorize what people buy in the marketplace by the attributes of what they've purchased. A lawn mower belongs in a different category from a hamburger, which belongs in a different category from a massage. But social psychologists often categorize what we purchase by our intent. Some things are *material purchases*—"made with the primary intention of acquiring . . . a tangible object that is kept in one's possession." Others are *experiential purchases*—"made with the primary intention of acquiring . . . an event or a series of events that one lives through."[15]

Several researchers have shown that people derive much greater satisfaction from purchasing experiences than they do from purchasing goods. When Leaf Van Boven of the University of Colorado at Boulder and Thomas Gilovich of Cornell University surveyed Americans and Canadians and asked them to reflect on what they'd bought recently, respondents overwhelmingly reported that experiential purchases made them happier than material purchases. Even when people ponder their *future* purchases, they expect that experiences will leave them more satisfied than physical goods.[16] Several factors explain this phenomenon. For instance, we adapt quickly to material changes. That spectacular new BMW that so delighted us three weeks ago is now just how we get to work. But that hike on Canada's West Coast Trail lingers in our mind—and as time goes by, we tend to forget the small-level annoyances (ticks) and remember the higher-level joys (amazing sunsets). Experiences also give us something to talk about and stories to tell, which can help us connect with others and deepen our own identities, both of which boost satisfaction.

As a result, framing a sale in experiential terms is more likely to lead to satisfied customers and repeat business. So if you're selling a car, go easy on emphasizing the rich Corinthian leather on the seats. Instead, point out what the car will allow the buyer to do—see new places, visit old friends, and add to a book of memories.

The label frame

If you've studied economics, lived through the Cold War, or played a few board games, you're probably familiar with the Prisoner's Dilemma. The basic scenario goes as follows: A and B have been arrested for a crime, but the police and prosecutors don't have sufficient evidence to convict them. So they decide to apply pressure by interrogating the two suspects separately. If A and B both keep mum, they each get only a light sentence—one month on unrelated charges. If they both confess, each will receive a six-month sentence. But if A confesses and B stays quiet, B gets ten years in prison and A walks free. Conversely, if B confesses and A stays quiet, A gets ten years in the slammer and B walks. Obviously, A and B would both be better off by cooperating—that is, by keeping their mouths shut. But if one party can't trust the other, he risks a lengthy prison stay if his partner betrays him—and that, in short, is the dilemma.

In 2004, social scientists from the Interdisciplinary Center in Israel, the U.S. Air Force Academy, and Stanford University recruited participants to play this game. But they changed the name. For one group, they called it the "Wall Street Game"; for the other, the "Community Game." Did a maneuver as innocuous as changing the label achieve results as significant as altering behavior?

Absolutely.

In the Wall Street Game, 33 percent of participants cooperated and went free. But in the Community Game, 66 percent reached that mutually beneficial result.[17] The label helped people answer the "Compared to what?" question. It put the exercise in context, hinted at what was expected, and changed behavior by a factor of two.

Something similar happened back in 1975 in three fifth-grade classrooms in the Chicago Public Schools. There a trio of Northwestern University researchers randomly assigned classrooms to three groups. Over a week, students in one group were told by teachers, janitors, and others that they were extremely neat—in fact, they had one of the neatest classrooms in their school. Children in the second group were simply used to be neat—told to pick up their trash, tidy their desks, and keep the classroom clean. The third group was the control. When investigators later measured the litter in the classrooms, and compared it with litter levels before the experiment began, the results were unmistakable. The neatest group by far was the first—the one that had been labeled "neat." Merely assigning that positive label—helping the students frame themselves in comparison with others—elevated their behavior.

The blemished frame

Can a negative ever be a positive when it comes to moving others? That's what three marketing professors investigated in a 2012 study. In one set of experiments, they presented information about a pair of hiking boots as if the study participants were shopping for them online. To half the group, researchers listed all the great things about the boots—orthopedic soles, waterproof material, a five-year warranty, and more. To the other half, they included the same list of positives, but followed it with a negative—these boots, unfortunately, came in only two colors. Remarkably, in many cases the people who'd gotten that small dose of negative information were *more likely* to purchase the boots than those who'd received the exclusively positive information.

The researchers dubbed this phenomenon the "blemishing effect"—where "adding a minor negative detail in an otherwise positive description of a target can give that description a more positive impact." But the blemishing effect seems to operate only under two circumstances. First, the people processing the information must be in what the researchers call a "low effort" state. That is, instead of focusing resolutely on the decision, they're proceeding with a little less effort—perhaps because they're busy or distracted. Second, the negative information must *follow* the positive information, not the reverse. Once again, the comparison creates clarity. "The core logic is that when individuals encounter weak negative information after already having received positive information, the weak negative information ironically highlights or increases the salience of the positive information."[18]

So if you're making your case to someone who's not intently weighing every single word, list all the positives—but do add a mild negative. Being honest about the existence of a small blemish can enhance your offering's true beauty.

The potential frame

So far we've looked at selling gourmet jam, German-language software, and a pair of awesome but slightly blemished hiking boots. But which frame is best when selling ourselves? Our initial, and very sensible, instinct is that we ought to use an achievement frame—and emphasize the deals we've done, the divisions we've turned around, the awards we've accumulated.

But in a fascinating and wide-ranging 2012 paper, Zakary Tormala and Jayson Jia of Stanford University and Michael Norton of the Harvard Business School suggest a different approach. What we really should do, they say, is emphasize our *potential*. For example, these researchers put participants in the role of a National Basketball Association general manager tasked with awarding contracts to players. Some participants had to offer a contract to a player with five years of experience who had produced some impressive stats. Others had to offer a contract to a rookie who was projected to produce those same statistics during his first five seasons of play. Participants, on average, gave the veteran player with solid numbers a salary of over four million dollars for his sixth year. But they said that for the rookie's sixth season, they'd expect to pay him more than *five* million dollars. Likewise, the researchers tested two different Facebook ads for the same comedian. Half the ads said the comedian, Kevin Shea, "could be the next big thing." The other half said, "He is the next big thing." The first ad generated far more click-throughs and likes than the second. The somewhat peculiar upshot of the research, the scholars write, is that "the potential to be good at something can be preferred over actually being good at that very same thing."[19]

People often find potential more interesting than accomplishment because it's more uncertain, the researchers argue. That uncertainty can lead people to think more deeply about the person they're evaluating—and the more intensive processing that requires can lead to generating more and better reasons why the person is a good choice. So next time you're selling yourself, don't fixate only on what you achieved yesterday. Also emphasize the promise of what you could accomplish tomorrow.

Finding an Off-ramp

Once you've found the problem and the proper frame, you have one more step. You need to give people an off-ramp.

A study about a college food drive illustrates this point. Students were asked to nominate two groups of peers—those "least likely" to contribute to a food drive and those "most likely" to do so. Then researchers divided each group in half. They sent half of the least likely group and half of the most likely group a letter, addressed to each of the students by name, asking them to donate a specific type of food and including a map showing where they could drop it off. A few days later, researchers gave these students a reminder phone call.

The other half of each group—again, half of the least likely group and half of the most likely—received a different letter. Researchers addressed it "Dear student" rather than to a specific person. The letter didn't ask for a particular kind of food and didn't include a map. These students didn't receive a reminder phone call, either.

What mattered more—the disposition of the students or the content of the letters?

Among the students in the least likely group who received the less detailed letter, a whopping 0 percent contributed to the food drive. But their counterparts, who were more disposed to giving but who'd received the same letter, didn't exactly wow researchers with their benevolence. Only 8 percent of them made a food donation.

However, the letter that gave students details on how to act had a huge effect. Twenty-five percent of students deemed least likely to contribute actually made a contribution when they received the letter with a concrete appeal, a map, and a location for donating. What moved them wasn't only the request itself, but that the requesters had provided them an off-ramp for getting to their destination. A specific request accompanied by a clear way to get it done ended up with the least likely group donating food at *three times* the rate of the most likely who hadn't been given a clear path of action.[20]

The lesson: Clarity on how to think without clarity on how to act can leave people unmoved.

This chapter is also an off-ramp of sorts. I hope you've seen in Part Two that the qualities necessary for sales and non-sales selling today—the new ABCs—include a keen mind, a deft touch, and a sense of possibility. They've shown you how to be. But you also need to know what to do. For that, once you've looked at the Clarity Sample Case, please turn to Part Three.

SAMPLE CASE

•————————————•

Clarity

Clarify others' motives with two "irrational" questions.

Michael Pantalon is a research scientist at the Yale School of Medicine and a leading authority on "motivational interviewing." This technique, which originated in therapy and counseling but has since spread to other realms, seeks to spark behavior change not by coercing people, promising them rewards, or threatening them with punishments, but by tapping their inner drives. And the most effective tools for excavating people's buried drives are questions.

However, for the purposes of moving others, all questions are not created equal, Pantalon says. "I've learned that rational questions are ineffective for motivating resistant people. Instead I've found that irrational questions actually motivate people better," he has written.

So suppose your daughter is hemming and hawing, delaying and denying, and generally resisting studying for a big end-of-the-year algebra test. Using Pantalon's approach, you wouldn't say,

"Young lady, you must study," or "Please, please, please study for the test." Instead, you'd ask her two questions.

Question 1. "On a scale of 1 to 10, with 1 meaning 'not the least bit ready' and 10 meaning 'totally ready,' how ready are you to study?"

After she offers her answer, move to:

Question 2. "Why didn't you pick a lower number?"
"This is the question that catches everybody off guard," Pantalon writes in his book *Instant Influence*. Asking why the number isn't *lower* is the catalyst. Most people who resist doing or believing something don't have a binary, off-on, yes-no position. So don't ask a binary, off-on, yes-no question. If your prospect has even a faint desire to move, Pantalon says, asking her to locate herself on that 1-to-10 scale can expose an apparent "No" as an actual "Maybe."

Even more important, as your daughter explains her reasons for being a 4 rather than a 3, she begins announcing her own reasons for studying. She moves from defending her current behavior to articulating why, at some level, she wants to behave differently. And that, says Pantalon, allows her to clarify her personal, positive, and intrinsic motives for studying, which increases the chances she actually will.

So, on a scale of 1 to 10, how ready are you to try Pantalon's two-question technique? And why isn't your number lower?

Try a jolt of the unfamiliar.

Clarity, we've learned, depends on comparison. But many times we become so rutted in our own ways that we scarcely notice what we're doing or why we're doing it—which can impair our ability to bring clarity to others. Sometimes, as Tufts University psychologist Sam Sommers says, "it takes the jolt of the unfamiliar to remind you just how blind you are to your regular surroundings."

So give yourself one of the following:

Mini Jolt: Sit on the opposite end of the conference table at your next meeting. Travel home from work using a different route from normal. Instead of ordering what you usually do at your favorite restaurant, choose the eleventh item on the menu.

Half Jolt: Spend a day immersed in an environment not typically your own. If you're a schoolteacher, hang out at a friend's law office. If you're an accountant, take an afternoon and spend it with a lifeguard or park ranger.

Full Jolt: Travel to another country, with a culture different from your own. You'll likely return jolted—and clarified.

Become a curator.

In the old days, our challenge was *accessing* information. These days, our challenge is *curating* it. To make sense of the world, for ourselves and those we hope to move, we must wade through a mass of material flowing at us every day—selecting what's relevant and discarding what's not. Trouble is, most of us don't have any method to attack the madness. Fortunately, Beth Kanter—an expert in nonprofits, technology, and social media—has created a three-step process for curation newbies.

1. *Seek.* Once you've defined the area in which you'd like to curate (for example, middle school education reform or the latest skateboard fashion trends or the virtues and vices of mortgage-backed securities), put together a list of the best sources of information. Then set aside time to scan those sources regularly. Kanter recommends at least fifteen minutes, two times a day. As you scan, gather the most interesting items.

2. *Sense.* Here's where you add the real value, by creating meaning out of the material you've assembled. This can be as simple as making an annotated list of Web links or even regularly maintaining your own blog. She recommends tending to this list of resources every day.

3. *Share.* Once you've collected the good stuff and organized it in a meaningful way, you're ready to share it with your colleagues, your prospects, or your entire social network. You can do this through a regular e-mail or your own newsletter, or by using Facebook, Twitter, or LinkedIn. As you share, you'll help others see their own situations in a new light and possibly reveal hidden problems that you can solve.

"Putting content curation into practice is part art form, part science, but mostly about daily practice," writes Kanter. For more, see her "Content Curation Primer": http://www.bethkanter.org/content -curation-101/.

Learn how to ask better questions.

In the new world of sales, being able to ask the right questions is more valuable than producing the right answers. Unfortunately, our schools often have the opposite emphasis. They teach us how to answer, but not how to ask. The folks at the Right Question Institute are trying to correct that imbalance. They've come up with a method that educators can use to help students learn to ask better questions—and that can assist even those of us who graduated back in the twentieth century.

Before your next sales call, or maybe in advance of that awkward upcoming meeting with your ex-spouse or annoying boss, give RQI's step-by-step Question Formulation Technique a try.

1. Produce your questions.

Generate a list of questions by writing down as many as you can think of, without stopping to judge, discuss, or answer any of them. Don't edit. Just write the questions that pop into your head. Change any statements to questions.

2. Improve your questions.

Go through your list of questions and categorize each one as either "closed-ended" (questions that can be answered with "yes" or "no," or just one word) or "open-ended" (questions that require an explanation and cannot be answered with "yes" or "no," or just one word). Then, looking over the two types of questions, think about the advantages and disadvantages of each variety. Finally, for a few closed-ended questions, create an open-ended one, and for a few open-ended questions, create a closed-ended one.

3. Prioritize your questions.

Choose your three most important questions. Think about why you chose them. Then edit them one more time so they are ultra-clear.

Through this process you can identify a trio of powerful questions that you can ask the person on the other side of the table. And those questions can help both of you clarify where you are and where you should be going. Find more information on this at: http://www.rightquestion.org.

Read these books.

Several books discuss some of the themes in this chapter—from framing arguments to finding problems to curating information. These are five of my favorites.

Influence: Science and Practice by Robert Cialdini. Cialdini has done more to advance the scholarship of persuasion than anyone in the world. This book is his classic. You need to read it. Seriously. Go get it now. His public workshops, which I've attended, are also excellent. More information at: http://www.influenceatwork.com.

Made to Stick: Why Some Ideas Survive and Others Die by Chip Heath and Dan Heath. The Heath brothers are worthy successors to Cialdini. Their first book, which came out in 2007, is a gem. It will teach you how to create messages that stick, through the principles of simplicity, unexpectedness, concreteness, credibility, emotions, and stories.

Switch by Chip Heath and Dan Heath. Three years after *Made to Stick*, the Heath brothers came out with another book that's equally good. This one is about change—which they'll tell you depends on the emotional elephant and the rational rider working in concert. (Trust me—it makes sense.)

Mindless Eating: Why We Eat More Than We Think by Brian Wansink. The opposite of clarity is murkiness. And murkiness's close cousin is mindlessness—the state of being unaware. Wansink shows how mindlessness allows us to fall prey to hidden persuaders that make us overeat without even knowing it.

Nudge: Improving Decisions About Health, Wealth, and Happiness by Richard H. Thaler and Cass R. Sunstein. Two professors harvest the field of behavioral economics to reveal how altering "choice architecture" can nudge people to make better decisions about their lives.

Ask the Five Whys.

Those of you with toddlers in the house are familiar with, and perhaps annoyed by, the constant why-why-why. But there's a reason the little people are constantly asking that question. They're trying to figure out how things work in the crazy world we live in. The folks at IDEO, the award-winning innovation and design firm, have taken a lesson from the under-five set in one of the methods they use to find design problems.

They call their technique "Five Whys." It works like this:

When you want to figure out what kind of problem someone has, ask a "Why?" question. Then, in response to the answer, ask another "Why?" And again and again, for a total of five whys.

Yes, it might annoy the person you're asking. But you might be surprised by what you uncover. As IDEO explains it, "This exercise forces people to examine and express the underlying reasons for their behavior and attitudes." And that can help you discover the hidden problems that most need solving.

Find the one percent.

A long time ago, when I was in law school, I took a course called "International Business Transactions," taught by a professor named Harold Hongju Koh. I don't remember much about the particulars of what we learned in class that semester—a few things about letters of credit, I think, and some stuff about the Foreign Corrupt Practices Act. But I've never forgotten something Professor Koh told our class one spring afternoon.

He said that in an attempt to understand the law—or, for that matter, just about anything—the key was to focus on what he termed the "one percent." Don't get lost in the crabgrass of details, he urged us. Instead, think about the essence of what you're exploring—the one percent that gives life to the other ninety-nine. Understanding that one percent, and being able to explain it to others, is the hallmark of strong minds and good attorneys.

Clarity operates by the same logic. Whether you're selling computers to a giant company or a new bedtime to your youngest child, ask yourself: "What's the one percent?" If you can answer that question, and convey it to others, they're likely to be moved.

Part Three

What to Do

7.

Pitch

In the fall of 1853, an American craftsman named Elisha Otis, who had found a solution to one of the era's toughest engineering problems, went looking for a grand stage to demonstrate his invention.

At the time, many American buildings had elevators. But the mechanics of how these crude contraptions worked—a combination of ropes, pulleys, and hope—hadn't changed much since the days of Archimedes. A thick cable pulled a platform up and down a shaft, which often worked well—unless the cable snapped, at which point the platform would crash to the ground and destroy the elevator's contents.

Otis had figured out a way around this defect. He attached a wagon spring to the platform and installed ratchet bars inside the shaft so that if the rope ever did snap, the wagon spring safety brake would activate automatically and prevent the elevator from plummeting. It was an invention with huge potential in saving money and lives, but Otis faced a skeptical and fearful public.

So he rented out the main exhibit hall of what was then New York City's largest convention center. On the floor of the hall he constructed an open elevator platform and a shaft in which the platform could rise and descend. One afternoon, he gathered convention-goers for a demonstration. He climbed onto the platform and directed an assistant to hoist the elevator to its top height, about three stories off the ground. Then, as he stood and gazed down at the crowd, Otis took an ax and slashed the rope that was suspending the elevator in midair.

The audience gasped. The platform fell. But in seconds, the safety brake engaged and halted the elevator's descent. Still alive and standing, Otis looked out at the shaken crowd and said, "All safe, gentlemen. All safe."[1]

The moment marked two firsts. It was the first demonstration of an elevator safe enough to carry people. (Otis, you might have guessed by now, went on to found the Otis Elevator Company.) And more important for our purposes, it was a simple, succinct, and effective way to convey a complex message in an effort to move others—the world's first elevator pitch.

In Part Two, we learned how to *be*—the three qualities necessary for sales and non-sales selling. Here in Part Three (Chapters 7, 8, and 9), I'll discuss what to *do* by focusing on three key abilities: to pitch, to improvise, and to serve. This chapter is about pitching—the ability to distill one's point to its persuasive essence, much as Otis did back in 1853. And to understand the dynamics of that process and the purpose of the pitch itself, the place to begin is Hollywood.

Lessons from Tinseltown

At the epicenter of the entertainment business is the pitch. Television and movie executives take meetings with writers and other creative types, who pitch them ideas for the next blockbuster film or hit TV series. Motion pictures themselves offer a glimpse of these sessions. "It's *Out of Africa* meets *Pretty Woman*," promises an eager writer in the Hollywood satire *The Player*. "It's like *The Gods Must Be Crazy* except the Coke bottle is an actress!" But what really goes on behind those studio walls is often a mystery, which is why two business school professors decided to helicopter behind the lines for a closer look.

Kimberly Elsbach of the University of California, Davis, and Roderick Kramer of Stanford University spent five years in the thick of the Hollywood pitch process. They sat in on dozens of pitch meetings, analyzed transcripts of pitching sessions, and interviewed screenwriters, agents, and producers. The award-winning study[2] they wrote for the *Academy of Management Journal* offers excellent guidance even for those of us on the living room side of the streaming video.

Their central finding was that the success of a pitch depends as much on the catcher as on the pitcher. In particular, Elsbach and Kramer discovered that beneath this elaborate ritual were two processes. In the first, the catcher (i.e., the executive) used a variety of physical and behavioral cues to quickly assess the pitcher's (i.e., the writer's) creativity. The catchers took passion, wit, and quirkiness as positive cues—and slickness, trying too hard, and offering lots of different ideas as negative ones. If the catcher categorized the pitcher as "uncreative" in the first few minutes, the meeting was essentially over even if it had not actually ended.

But for pitchers, landing in the creative category wasn't enough, because a second process was at work. In the most successful pitches, the pitcher didn't push her idea on the catcher until she extracted a yes. Instead, she invited in her counterpart as a collaborator. The more the executives—often derided by their supposedly more artistic counterparts as "suits"—were able to contribute, the better the idea often became, and the more likely it was to be green-lighted. The most valuable sessions were those in which the catcher "becomes so fully engaged by a pitcher that the process resembles a mutual collaboration," the researchers found.[3] "Once the catcher feels like a creative collaborator, the odds of rejection diminish," Elsbach says.[4] Some of the study's subjects had their own way of describing these dynamics. One Oscar-winning producer told the professors, "At a certain point the writer needs to pull back as the creator of the story. And let [the executive] project what he needs onto your idea that makes the story whole for him." However, "in an unsuccessful pitch," another producer explained, "the person just doesn't yield or doesn't listen well."[5]

The lesson here is critical: The purpose of a pitch isn't necessarily to move others immediately to adopt your idea. The purpose is to offer something so compelling that it begins a conversation, brings the other person in as a participant, and eventually arrives at an outcome that appeals to both of you. In a world where buyers have ample information and an array of choices, the pitch is often the first word, but it's rarely the last.

The Six Successors to the Elevator Pitch

Elisha Otis's breakthrough had a catalytic effect on many industries, including the business of giving advice. Almost from the moment that elevators became commonplace, gurus like Dale Carnegie advised us to be ever ready with our "elevator speech." The idea was that if you found yourself stepping into an elevator and encountering the big boss, you needed to be able to explain who you were and what you did between the time the doors closed shut and dinged back open at your floor.

For several decades during the twentieth century, the elevator pitch was standard operating procedure. But times and technology change. In the twenty-first century, this well-worn practice has grown a bit threadbare for at least two reasons. First, organizations today are generally more democratic than they were in the stratified world of the gray flannel suit. Many CEOs, even in large companies, sit in cubicles like everyone else or in open floor plans that allow contact and collaboration. The closed door is less and less the norm. Fifty years ago, the only chance you or I might get to communicate with the company CEO was at the elevator. Today, we can swing by her workstation, send her an e-mail, or ask her a question at an all-hands meeting. Second, when that mid-twentieth-century CEO stepped off the elevator and returned to his office, he probably had a few phone calls, memos, and meetings to contend with. Nowadays, everyone—whether we're the head of an organization or its freshest hire—faces a torrent of information. The McKinsey Global Institute estimates that the typical American hears or reads more than one hundred thousand words every day.[6] If we leave our desk for a few minutes to grab a cup of coffee, greeting us upon our return will be new e-mails, texts, and tweets—not to mention all the blog posts we haven't read, videos we haven't watched, and, if we're over forty, phone calls we haven't returned.

Today, we have more opportunities to get out our message than Elisha Otis ever imagined. But our recipients have far more distractions than those conventioneers in 1853 who assembled to watch Otis not fall to his death. As a result, we need to broaden our repertoire of pitches for an age of limited attention and *caveat venditor.*

Over the last few years, I've been collecting pitches anywhere I could find them. Based on my research, here are six promising successors to the elevator pitch—what they are, why they work, and how you can use them to begin a conversation that leads to moving others.

1. The one-word pitch

The ultimate pitch for an era of short attention spans begins with a single word—and doesn't go any further.

The one-word pitch derives in part from Maurice Saatchi, who, with his brother Charles, founded the advertising agencies Saatchi & Saatchi and M&C Saatchi. For several years, Saatchi has been touting what he calls "one-word equity." He argues that a world populated with "digital natives"—those under age thirty who scarcely remember life without the Internet—has intensified the battle for attention in ways no one has fully comprehended. Attention spans aren't merely shrinking, he says. They're nearly disappearing. And the only way to be heard is to push brevity to its breaking point.

"In this model, companies compete for global ownership of one word in the public mind," Saatchi writes. The companies' aim, and the aim of this type of pitch, is "to define the one characteristic they most want associated with their brand around the world, and then own it. That is one-word equity."[7]

When anybody thinks of you, they utter that word. When anybody utters that word, they think of you.

If this aspiration seems fanciful, consider how far some companies have moved in this direction. Ask yourself: What technology company do you think of when you hear the word "search"? What credit card company comes to mind when you hear the word "priceless"? If you answered Google for the former and MasterCard for the latter, you've made Saatchi's case.

"Nowadays only brutally simple ideas get through," he says. "They travel lighter, they travel faster." And although Saatchi labels his own concept with two words glued together by a hyphen and followed by a third, he insists that brutal simplicity requires one—and only one—word. "Two words is not God. It is two gods, and two gods are one too many."[8]

It's easy to dismiss the one-word pitch as more simplistic than simple—the ultimate dumbing-down of a message. But that misunderstands both the process of formulating a one-word pitch and the galvanizing effect of its introduction. Reducing your point to that single word demands discipline and forces clarity. Choose the proper word, and the rest can fall into place. For example, in his 2012 reelection campaign, President Barack Obama built his entire strategy around one word: "Forward." Its use yields an important lesson for your own pitch.

One.

2. The question pitch

In 1980, Ronald Reagan was running for president of the United States in a grim economy. Unseating an incumbent, even one as vulnerable as then president Jimmy Carter, who'd been elected in 1976, is never easy. So Reagan had to make the case that Carter's poor stewardship of the economy required the country to change leadership. In his pitch to voters, Reagan could have delivered a declarative statement: "Your economic situation has deteriorated over the last forty-eight months." And he could have supported the assertion with a slew of data on the nation's spiraling inflation and steep unemployment. Instead, Reagan asked a question: "Are you better off now than you were four years ago?"

As we saw in Chapter 5 with interrogative self-talk, questions often pack a surprising punch. Yet they're underused when we try to move others, despite a raft of social science that suggests we should deploy them more often. Beginning with research in the 1980s, several scholars have found that questions can outperform statements in persuading others. For example, Robert Burnkrant and Daniel Howard of Ohio State University tested the potency of a series of short pitches to a group of undergraduates. At issue was whether universities should require seniors to pass a comprehensive exam as a condition of graduation. When the researchers presented strong arguments for the policy as questions (e.g., "Will passing a comprehensive exam be an aid to those who seek admission to graduate and professional schools?"), the participants were much likelier to support the policy than they were when presented with the equivalent argument as a statement. However, questions weren't always best. The researchers also found that when the underlying arguments were *weak*, presenting them in the interrogative form had a *negative* effect.[9]

The reasons for the difference go to the core of how questions operate. When I make a statement, you can receive it passively. When I ask a question, you're compelled to respond, either aloud if the question is direct or silently if the question is rhetorical. That requires at least a modicum of effort on your part or, as the researchers put it, "more intensive processing of message content."[10] Deeper processing reveals the stolidity of strong arguments and the flimsiness of weak ones. In the 1980 example, then, the question that worked so well for Reagan would have been disastrous for Carter. If he were trying to argue that Americans' economic conditions had improved during his presidency—when for the vast majority of voters they had not—asking them "Are you better off now than you were four years ago?" would have prompted people to think more deeply, leading most to a conclusion different from what Carter might have intended. Likewise, in 2012 when Republican presidential nominee Mitt Romney tried to use Reagan's question in his race against Obama, the tactic didn't work very well. Subsequent polling discovered that while many voters did believe they were worse off than they were four years prior, a greater percentage said they were better off or the same,[11] dulling some of the sharpness of this line of attack.

By making people work just a little harder, question pitches prompt people to come up with *their own* reasons for agreeing (or not). And when people summon their own reasons for believing something, they endorse the belief more strongly and become more likely to act on it. So given your knowledge of the underlying social psychology, the next time you've got a strong case to make to a prospective employer, new sales prospect, or undecided friend, do you think you should skip making a statement and instead ask a question?

3. The rhyming pitch

Lawyers, especially trial lawyers, are in the moving business. They sell juries on verdicts. And integral to their efforts is their closing argument—the final summary of all the evidence that's been presented over the course of the trial. It's the ultimate pitch, days and sometimes weeks of material reduced to its essentials.

In 1995, an American lawyer named Johnnie L. Cochran presented his closing argument in the trial of his client, the former football star O. J. Simpson, who stood accused of murdering his ex-wife and her friend. Among the evidence the jurors had to consider was a bloodstained glove found at the murder scene that prosecutors said belonged to Simpson. To demonstrate that the glove was indeed his, during the trial, prosecutors had asked Simpson to slip it on in front of the jury. Simpson tried, but struggled—and failed to get the glove on. In his closing statement, Cochran made the following pitch for his client's innocence: "If it doesn't fit . . ."

Most Americans who were alive at the time know the rest: ". . . you must acquit." The jury exonerated Simpson—and one reason was Cochran's seven-word rhyme: If it doesn't fit, you must acquit.

Cochran, who died in 2005, was probably operating on instinct and experience, but his technique has ample support in the social science literature. For instance, in a 2000 study, Matthew S. McGlone and Jessica Tofighbakhsh of Lafayette College presented participants with a list of sixty aphorisms and asked them to rate whether each was "an accurate description of human behavior."[12] Researchers included existing aphorisms that rhymed along with modified versions that did not, as you can see on the next page.

Original, rhyming version	Modified, nonrhyming version
Woes unite foes.	Woes unite enemies.
What sobriety conceals, alcohol reveals.	What sobriety conceals, alcohol unmasks.
Life is mostly strife.	Life is mostly struggle.
Caution and measure will win you treasure.	Caution and measure will win you riches.

Participants rated the aphorisms in the left column as far more accurate than those in the right column, even though each pair says essentially the same thing. Yet when the researchers asked people, "In your opinion, do aphorisms that rhyme describe human behavior more accurately than those that do not rhyme?" the overwhelming answer was no. Participants were attributing accuracy to the rhyming versions *unconsciously*. Only when they were explicitly instructed to disentangle the meaning from the form did they rate the statements as equally accurate.[13]

What's going on? Rhymes boost what linguists and cognitive scientists call "processing fluency," the ease with which our minds slice, dice, and make sense of stimuli. Rhymes taste great and go down easily and we equate that smoothness with accuracy. In this way, rhyme can enhance reason.

That's one explanation for why Haribo, the German candy company best known for its "gummy bears," uses a rhyming pitch in every country where it operates and in each of those countries' languages.

For example, its pitch in English is: *"Kids and grown-ups love it so—the happy world of Haribo."*

In French it's: *"Haribo, c'est beau la vie—pour les grands et les petits."*

In Spanish it's: *"Haribo, dulces sabores—para pequeños y mayores."*

Haribo is acting on knowledge that you, too, can use in your work and life. If you're testifying before your city council, summarizing your main point with a rhyme gives council members a way to talk about your proposal when they deliberate. If you're one of a series of freelancers invited to make a presentation before a big potential client, including a rhyme can enhance the processing fluency of your listeners, allowing your message to stick in their minds when they compare you and your competitors. Remember: Pitches that rhyme are more sublime.

4. The subject-line pitch

E-mail has become so integrated into our lives that, as Xerox PARC researchers describe, it has "become more like a habitat than an application."[14] But as with any habitat, the more deeply we're immersed in it, the less we notice its distinctive features. That's why many of us haven't realized that every e-mail we send is a pitch. It's a plea for someone's attention and an invitation to engage.

Whether somebody accepts that invitation, or even opens the e-mail at all, depends most on who sent it. You're more likely to look at a message from your boss or your girlfriend than from a company you've never heard of promising a product you'll never need. But the next most important element in e-mail engagement is the subject line—the headline that previews and promises what the message contains.

In 2011 three Carnegie Mellon University professors conducted a series of studies examining why some subject lines are more effective than others. In one experiment, they used the "think-aloud method," wherein participants worked through their e-mail inboxes and narrated their decisions about what they read, replied to, forwarded, or deleted. The researchers discovered that participants based their decisions on two factors: utility and curiosity. People were quite likely to "read emails that directly affected their work." No surprise there. But they were also likely "to open messages when they had moderate levels of uncertainty about the contents, i.e. they were 'curious' what the messages were about."[15]

Utility and curiosity were about equally potent, but they seemed to operate independently of each other. Utility worked better when recipients had lots of e-mail, but "curiosity [drove] attention to email under conditions of low demand." One explanation for the different behaviors under different conditions was the motives behind each choice. People opened useful messages for extrinsic reasons; they had something to gain or lose. They opened the other messages for intrinsic reasons; they were just curious. Ample research has shown that trying to add intrinsic motives on top of extrinsic ones often backfires.[16] As a result, say the Carnegie Mellon researchers, your e-mail subject line should be either obviously useful (*Found the best & cheapest photocopier*) or mysteriously intriguing (*A photocopy breakthrough!*), but probably not both (*The Canon IR2545 is a photocopy breakthrough*). And considering the volume of e-mail most people contend with, usefulness will often trump intrigue, although tapping recipients' inherent curiosity, in the form of a provocative or even blank subject line, can be surprisingly effective in some circumstances.

Along with utility and curiosity is a third principle: specificity. Indeed, Brian Clark, founder of the popular Copyblogger copywriting website, recommends that subject lines should be "ultra-specific."[17] Thus a mushy subject line like *Improve your golf swing* achieves less than one offering *4 tips to improve your golf swing this afternoon.*

Tapping the principles of utility, curiosity, and specificity, if I were to send you an e-mail pitch about the preceding five paragraphs, I might use this subject line if I suspected your inbox was jammed: *3 simple but proven ways to get your e-mail opened.* But if I thought you had a lighter e-mail load, and you already knew me well, I might use: *Some weird things I just learned about e-mail.*

5. The Twitter pitch

Each year the Tippie College of Business at the University of Iowa receives more than three hundred applications for roughly seventy spots in the coming year's MBA program. Applicants submit their university grades, scores on the standardized business school admission test, letters of recommendation, and several essays. But in 2011, Tippie added a contest to its process, one intended to test the pitching prowess of the future business leaders it would be educating. The school asked a fairly standard essay question: "What makes you an exceptional Tippie full-time M.B.A. candidate and future M.B.A. hire?" But it told applicants to respond in the form of a tweet—a micro-message of 140 or fewer characters.[18]

Meet the Twitter pitch, which uses Twitter as a platform and its character count as a limit on loquaciousness. One of the pioneers of this form is Stowe Boyd, a programmer, designer, and investor. In 2008 Boyd was heading to a conference and planning to meet with some start-up companies. To avoid getting buried beneath a sandstorm of eager entrepreneurs, he required any start-up seeking a meeting to send him its pitch via Twitter. This approach, said one commentator, is "quick, painless, and to-the-point. It cuts through the PR babble and forces companies to summarize what they do in 140 characters or less."[19] As Twitter insinuates itself more deeply into our lives, Boyd's "twitpitch" has become another important tool in everyone's persuasion kit.

The mark of an effective tweet, like the mark of any effective pitch, is that it engages recipients and encourages them to take the conversation further—by responding, clicking a link, or sharing the tweet with others. The few scholars who have studied this new medium with any rigor have found that only a small category of tweets actually accomplish those goals. In 2011, three computer scientists from Carnegie Mellon, MIT, and Georgia Tech undertook the first systematic look at what they call "microblog content value." They set up a website called Who Gives a Tweet and invited Twitter users to rate other people's tweets in exchange for subjecting their own tweets to reader evaluations. After analyzing more than forty-three thousand ratings, the investigators found a communications medium that a secondary school guidance counselor would say wasn't living up to its potential. Readers rated only 36 percent of tweets as worth reading, a surprisingly low figure considering that they were evaluating tweets from people they'd chosen to follow. They described 25 percent as not worth reading at all. And they rated 39 percent as neutral, which, given the volume of our daily distractions, is tantamount to declaring those, too, not worth reading at all.[20]

The types of tweets with the lowest ratings fell into three categories: Complaints ("My plane is late. Again."); Me Now ("I'm about to order a tuna sandwich"); and Presence Maintenance ("Good morning, everyone!").[21] But three of the categories rated the highest provide some insight on pitching via this new medium. For instance, readers assigned the highest ratings to tweets that asked questions of followers, confirming once again the power of the interrogative to engage and persuade. They prized tweets that provided information and links, especially if the material was fresh and new and offered the sort of clarity discussed in Chapter 6. And they gave high ratings to self-promoting tweets—those ultimate sales pitches—provided that the tweet offered useful information as part of the promotion.[22]

Which leads back to the University of Iowa's venture into Twitter self-promotion. The winner of that first contest was John Yates, who crafted his winning entry in the form of a haiku (even including the syllable count of each line) to emphasize his previous work experience in Asia:

> Globally minded (5)
> Innovative and driven (7)
> Tippie can sharpen (5).

No, it doesn't make one's heart swell. But it's engaging and provides relevant information. And it secured the applicant a spot in Tippie's incoming class, along with a scholarship package worth more than $37,000. Given his ability to earn more than $600 per character, and more than $3,000 per syllable, young Mr. Yates might have a future in the new world of selling.

6. The Pixar pitch

Four hundred miles north of Hollywood, in a small city along the eastern edge of San Francisco Bay, sits the headquarters of an unlikely entertainment colossus. Pixar Animation Studios, in Emeryville, California, opened in 1979 as the geeky computer graphics division of Lucasfilm. Thirty-five years later, it's one of the most successful studios in movie history. Starting with *Toy Story* in

1995, Pixar has produced thirteen feature films that together have grossed $7.6 billion worldwide, an astonishing $585 million per movie.[23] Six Pixar films—*Finding Nemo, The Incredibles, Ratatouille, WALL-E, Up,* and *Toy Story 3*—have won the Academy Award for Best Animated Feature, just a few of the twenty-six total Oscars the studio has taken home.

How does Pixar do it? Success has many parents—the foresight of Steve Jobs, who invested in the company early; the distribution and marketing muscle of the Walt Disney Company, which struck a development deal with the studio early on and acquired it in 2006; the meticulous attention to detail for which Pixar's army of technical and artistic talent is renowned. But an additional reason might be the stories themselves.

Emma Coats, a former story artist at the studio, has cracked the Pixar code—and, in the process, created a template for an irresistible new kind of pitch. Coats has argued that every Pixar film shares the same narrative DNA, a deep structure of storytelling that involves six sequential sentences:

Once upon a time _____.
Every day, _____. *One day* _____
_____. *Because of that,* _____.
Because of that, _____. *Until finally*
_____.

Take, for example, the plot of *Finding Nemo*:

<u>Once upon a time</u> there was a widowed fish named Marlin who was extremely protective of his only son, Nemo. <u>Every day</u>, Marlin warned Nemo of the ocean's dangers and implored him not to swim far away. <u>One day</u> in an act of

defiance, Nemo ignores his father's warnings and swims into the open water. <u>Because of that</u>, he is captured by a diver and ends up as a pet in the fish tank of a dentist in Sydney. <u>Because of that</u>, Marlin sets off on a journey to recover Nemo, enlisting the help of other sea creatures along the way. <u>Until finally</u> Marlin and Nemo find each other, reunite, and learn that love depends on trust.[24]

This six-sentence format is both appealing and supple. It allows pitchers to take advantage of the well-documented persuasive force of stories[25]—but within a framework that forces conciseness and discipline.

Imagine you're a nonprofit organization that's created a home HIV test and you're looking for funders. Your Pixar pitch could go something like this:

<u>Once upon a time</u> there was a health crisis haunting many parts of Africa. <u>Every day</u>, thousands of people would die of AIDS and HIV-related illness, often because they didn't know they carried the virus. <u>One day</u> we developed an inexpensive home HIV kit that allowed people to test themselves with a simple saliva swab. <u>Because of that</u>, more people got tested. <u>Because of that</u>, those with the infection sought treatment and took measures to avoid infecting others. <u>Until finally</u> this menacing disease slowed its spread and more people lived longer lives.

It's even possible to summarize this book with a Pixar pitch:

<u>Once upon a time</u> only some people were in sales. <u>Every day</u>, they sold stuff, we did stuff, and everyone was happy.

<u>One day</u> everything changed: All of us ended up in sales—and sales changed from a world of *caveat emptor* to *caveat venditor*. <u>Because of that</u>, we had to learn the new ABCs—attunement, buoyancy, and clarity. <u>Because of that</u>, we had to learn some new skills—to pitch, to improvise, and to serve. <u>Until finally</u> we realized that selling isn't some grim accommodation to a brutal marketplace culture. It's part of who we are—and therefore something we can do better by being more human.

To see each of the six pitches in action, imagine that you live in the fictional town of Beeston. The bridge that spans the nearby Girona River and connects your town to the larger city of Arborville has grown rickety—and you're leading a citizen campaign to replace the structure with a modern four-lane bridge. You've got many people to persuade—the town government, the citizens of Beeston, maybe even people in Arborville. And you'll need to do considerable work, figuring out how to finance the bridge, assessing its environmental impact, deciding who will design and construct it, and so on. But each of the six pitches offers a way to begin the conversations that will lead to the outcome you seek.

Your Pixar pitch, for instance, could be:

<u>Once upon a time</u> it was difficult and time-consuming to get from Beeston to Arborville. <u>Every day</u>, people tried to cross the old bridge, but it took them a long time and some didn't even bother because of the delays and safety concerns. <u>One day</u> citizens came together to finance and build a new, modern bridge. <u>Because of that</u>, people in Beeston wasted less time and their families felt safer. <u>Be-</u>

<u>cause of that</u>, more were able to work and shop in Arborville, which helped that economy flourish. <u>Until finally</u> the new bridge became such a fixture in our lives that we wondered why we had waited so long to build it.

Your Twitter pitch could include an online link to an artist's rendering of the bridge along with a list of its benefits and entice people to click it with: *See what tomorrow's Beeston and Arborville can look like & why we need to create that future.*

If you're sending information to your fellow Beeston citizens, your subject line pitch could be: *3 reasons why Beeston families support a new bridge.*

Your rhyming pitch? *Opportunities are wide on the other side.*

Your question pitch could help people think through their own experiences: *Should it be such a pain to get to Arborville?*

And your one-word pitch could explain the reason for your efforts (not to mention an indispensable lesson of this chapter): *Connect.*

SAMPLE CASE

Pitch

Practice your six pitches.

There are three ways to learn and perfect the six pitches: Practice, practice, practice. Here's a place to begin. (You can also find extra copies of this practice sheet at http://www.danpink.com/pitch.)

1. The One-Word Pitch

Pro tip: Write a fifty-word pitch. Reduce it to twenty-five words. Then to six words. One of those remaining half-dozen is almost certainly your one-word pitch.

    Your try: _____.

2. The Question Pitch

Pro tip: Use this if your arguments are strong. If they're weak, make a statement. Or better yet, find some new arguments.

    Your try: _____?

3. The Rhyming Pitch

Pro tip: Don't rack your brain for rhymes. Go online and find a rhyming dictionary. I'm partial to RhymeZone (http://www.rhymezone.com).

Your try: _____.

4. The Subject Line Pitch

Pro tip: Review the subject lines of the last twenty e-mail messages you've sent. Note how many of them appeal to either utility or curiosity. If that number is less than ten, rewrite each one that fails the test.

Your try: _____.

5. The Twitter Pitch

Pro tip: Even though Twitter allows 140 characters, limit your pitch to 120 characters so that others can pass it on. Remember: The best pitches are short, sweet, and easy to retweet.

Your try: _____.

6. The Pixar Pitch

Pro tip: Read all twenty-two of former Pixar story artist Emma Coats's story rules: http://bit.ly/jlVWrG

Your try: Once upon a time _____.
Every day, _____. One day _____.
Because of that, _____. Because of
that, _____. Until finally _____.

Answer three key questions.

As you prepare your pitch, whichever variety you choose, clarify your purpose and strategy by making sure you can answer these three questions:

After someone hears your pitch . . .

1. What do you want them to *know?*
2. What do you want them to *feel?*
3. What do you want them to *do?*

If you've got strong answers to these three questions, the pitch will come together more easily.

Collect other people's pitches and record your own.

How do artists get better at their craft? They practice, of course. But they also pay attention. A painter visits galleries to view other artists' work and to make notes about their technique. A singer records an early version of a song, listens to it several times, and devises ways to improve it. Pitches are an art form of their own, so you, too, should act like an artist.

For example, keep a pitch notebook. With a small notepad or on your smartphone, jot down the great pitches you hear as you're moving through the world—a shrewd advertising tagline, a mom's request to her kid, a colleague's plea for a new assignment. This exercise serves two purposes. It will make you aware of all the pitches in your midst. And it will help you see which techniques move others and which merely drift into the wind.

Also, try recording your practice pitches. Call yourself and leave a voice mail with your pitch or dictate it using a smartphone dictation app. Then listen. Does what you're saying make sense? How's your tone? Your rate of speech? Listening to your own voice can be painful, but it's a smart way to practice—and to spare yourself even more pain in the future.

Add a visual.

It's the saying every writer detests: "A picture is worth a thousand words." Although this aphorism doesn't rhyme, it still contains a few morsels of truth. In almost every pitch, the main ingredients are words—or in the case of one type, *a* word—but you can flavor certain varieties with images. For example, you can enliven question pitches, one-word pitches, and rhyming pitches by accompanying them with a single photograph or illustration that captures your idea. As digital communication relies less on text and more on images, your subject line and Twitter pitches can link to a compelling visual. You can even use props. For instance, if George Akerlof, the economist I discussed in Chapter 3, were pitching his idea about the cascading consequences of information asymmetry, he might hold up a lemon.

Likewise, video offers a way to combine the efficiency of electronic communication with the intimacy of seeing another person's face and hearing her voice. One excellent technique on this front is sending short video messages by e-mail, which you can do almost effortlessly, and usually for free, on QuickTime (get the details at: http://www.quicktime.com).

Experiment with *pecha-kucha*.

PowerPoint is like the weather or reality TV: Everybody complains about it, but nobody does anything about it. No matter where we work or learn, we must endure the blatherings of people who anesthetize us with bullet points and then, in the dark of a conference room, steal our souls and bake them into 3-D pie charts.

Three cheers, then, to Mark Dytham and Astrid Klein, Tokyo-based architects who've brewed an antidote to awful PowerPoint presentations. They call their creation *pecha-kucha*,* which is Japanese for "chatter."

A *pecha-kucha* presentation contains twenty slides, each of which appears on the screen for twenty seconds. That's it. The rules are rigid, which is the point. It's not nineteen slides or twenty-one seconds. It's 20 x 20. Presenters make their pitch in six minutes and forty seconds of perfectly timed words and images. Then they shut up and sit down. The format promotes clarity through constraints. And because the slides advance automatically, presenters must convey their message with both elegance and speed.

Since its introduction in 2003, *pecha-kucha* has spread like a benevolent virus and metamorphosed into an international movement. Several organizations now use it for internal presentations. And Klein and Dytham have established a foundation that operates free PechaKucha Nights in 547 cities around the world. Visit

---

*It's pronounced "puh-CHOCK-chuh."

one to see how it's done. Then try it yourself. For more information, go to http://www.pecha-kucha.org.

Pay attention to sequence and numbers.

The social science literature is full of interesting (and sometimes contradictory) findings about how sequence and numbers affect pitches. Here are two general rules that are backed by sound evidence. (I've included a link to the research papers themselves for those who want to dig deeper.)

1. *Go first if you're the incumbent, last if you're the challenger.*
   In competitive sales presentations, where a series of
   sellers make their pitches one after another, the
   market leader is most likely to get selected if it
   presents first, according to Virginia Tech University
   researchers. But for a challenger, the best spot, by
   far, is to present last (http://bit.ly/NRpdp6). How
   widely this applies to other settings isn't clear from
   the research, but in general, the middle is the place
   you're most likely to get run over.
2. *Granular numbers are more credible than coarse numbers.*
   A University of Michigan study asked participants to
   estimate the battery life of two GPS devices. One
   device claimed to have a battery life of "up to 2
   hours"; the other had an identical, but more finely
   grained claim of "up to 120 minutes." Participants
   estimated the first battery would last 89 minutes, but
   the second would last longer—106 minutes (http://
   bit.ly/yapcPA).

Ask people to describe your invisible pitch in three words.

We don't always realize it, but what we do and how we do it are themselves pitches. We're conveying a message about ourselves, our work, or our organization—and other people are interpreting it.

Take some time to find out what they think you're saying. Recruit ten people—a combination of coworkers and friends and family. Then ask them which three words come to mind in response to one of these questions: *What is my company about? What is my product or service about? What am I about?* Make it clear that you're not asking them for physical qualities ("tall, dark, and handsome") but something deeper.

Once you gather these words, look for patterns. Many people are surprised by the disconnect between what they think they're conveying and what others are actually hearing. Knowing is the prelude to improving.

8.

Improvise

On a sleepy Tuesday morning in late spring, I find myself in a
weird and compromising position: I'm on the fourteenth
floor of a Manhattan office building, standing toe to toe with
a woman who's not my wife and staring deeply into her eyes.

Don't blame me for this transgression. Blame my ears. Like
most of you, I've had a well-matched set of ears my whole life. But
like many of you, I was never really taught how to use them. So
I've come to this strange setting, a narrow conference room with
windows covered by plain brown paper, to learn how to listen. And
like the thirteen executives here with me—they hail from large
companies like Bank of America and from digital start-ups with
oddly spelled names—I've come to study with a master. Her name
is Cathy Salit. Back in 1970, she dropped out of eighth grade and
started her own school on Manhattan's Upper West Side. That led
to a career as a community organizer and then to one as an actor
and then, with a few peculiar twists, to her current position as
something of a sales whisperer.

She runs a company called Performance of a Lifetime, which teaches businesspeople improvisational theater—not to secure them low-paying gigs in drafty Greenwich Village clubs, but to make them more effective in their regular jobs. And at the heart of what she teaches is listening.

As I wait for Salit's session to begin, one of my fellow students— he wears glasses and his lower lip juts out in front of his upper one—asks me where I work.

"I'm a writer," I say, inviting the conversation with false cheer. "I work for myself."

He turns away and doesn't talk to me again. Seems like this guy needs help on listening. (Or perhaps I need to reread the chapter on pitching.)

So when the time comes to partner up for the first exercise, I avoid him and instead approach a slim and stylish woman about my age. She's a top executive at a major cosmetics company—and looks the part. Four-inch heels that enclose dainty feet whose toenails are painted slate gray. Tan pants and a sheer, ruffled blue blouse. Platinum hair pulled back into a tight ballerina's bun.

We stand facing each other, my unshaven chin only inches from her tiny porcelain nose. Our first lesson, Salit says, is "the mirror exercise." We look our partner in the eye and match her every movement as if we're gazing at ourselves in the mirror.

My partner slowly raises her right hand—so I slowly raise my left hand. She lifts her left hand, showing me her palm. I raise my right hand to the same level and turn the palm outward. Her head turns right. Mine, on cue, goes left. Legs lift. Shoulders shrug. Knees bend. All together.

It's awfully close and a little awkward. To be forced into such intimacy with an unattractive stranger is excruciating—or so I imagine she's thinking.

Then Salit dings a bell—the kind you'd find at the front desk of the Bates Motel—and it's my turn to lead. I place my arms akimbo. Her thin arms match the pose. I widen my stance. So does she. I clasp my fingers together and raise them above my head. She does the same. I pivot my body clockwise. She . . . I can tell you're getting this now.

As we learned in Chapter 4, strategic mimicry can enhance perspective-taking. But the mirroring we're doing here has a different purpose. Salit is teaching us the techniques of improvisational theater—which, it turns out, are critical for anyone who wants to move others.

Sales and theater have much in common. Both take guts. Salespeople pick up the phone and call strangers; actors walk onto the stage in front of them. Both invite rejection—for salespeople, slammed doors, ignored calls, and a pile of nos; for actors, a failed audition, an unresponsive audience, a scathing review. And both have evolved along comparable trajectories.

Theater, for instance, has always relied on scripts. Actors have discretion to interpret material their own way, but the play tells them what to say and, in many cases, how and where to say it. America's sales pioneers sought to replicate theater's staged approach. One of the titans, John H. Patterson, who founded the National Cash Register Company in the late 1800s, required all of NCR's salesmen to memorize scripts. Over time, as Harvard University business historian Walter Friedman has written, these scripts grew more detailed—morphing from a short primer called "How I Sell National Cash Registers" into a sales manual that ran nearly two hundred pages.[1] The ever more detailed instructions, Friedman says, focused "not only on what salesmen should say, but also on what they were to do while saying it," complete with NCR's version of stage directions. Sprinkled into the company-crafted monologues were asterisks "that indicated that the salesman was supposed to point to the item he was referring to"—as in *Now, sir, this register* makes the entries. The indication* of the transaction shows through this glass.**[2] Patterson and his crew even produced a *Book of Arguments* so that if customers raised questions or concerns, its salesmen could respond with well-rehearsed lines.

The NCR way—carefully scripted mini-dramas leading to a happy ending for the seller—dominated sales around the world for most of the twentieth century. And it remains part of the modern landscape—with sales organizations devising elaborate processes and audience-tested phrases to guide their players toward the final curtain. Scripts perform nicely in stable and predictable environments—when buyers have minimal choices and sellers have maximal information. But those circumstances, as we've seen, have become rarer. A memorized *Book of Arguments* is less valuable when the company already provides a list of "Frequently Asked Questions" on its website and when, in any event, customers can discover the ground truth from their social networks.

Here theater offers some instruction on what comes next. For hundreds of years, except for the occasional clown or mime, most stage performances relied on actors reciting memorized lines written by someone else. Indeed, until 1968, the Lord Chamberlain's office in the United Kingdom had to read and approve every play before it could be performed in the UK—and sent monitors to watch the plays to ensure performers were sticking to the approved text.[3]

But about fifty years ago, two innovators began to challenge the single-minded reliance on scripts. The first was Viola Spolin, an American who in the 1940s and 1950s developed a set of games— first for children, then for professional actors—centered on improvising characters, speeches, and scenes. In 1963, she wrote a book,

Improvisation for the Theater, that encapsulated these exercises and quickly became a mainstay of theater programs. Thanks to her son, Paul Sills, who took up the family trade, her ideas eventually gave rise to the now legendary Second City troupe—whose alumni (from John Belushi to Stephen Colbert to Tina Fey) have shaped American popular entertainment with their mastery of off-script, real-time comedic performance.

The second innovator was Keith Johnstone, a Brit who worked for years at London's Royal Court Theatre. As he grew weary of conventional theater he, too, began devising his own set of looser, less traditional performance techniques. And in 1979 he wrote what many consider the seminal work in the field, *Impro: Improvisation and the Theatre*. (The founders of Palantir, a company I mentioned in Chapter 2, ask all employees to read *Impro* before starting their jobs.)

By encouraging directors and performers to recognize the virtues of breaking with the script, Spolin and Johnstone helped make improv a mainstream form of entertainment. Sales and non-sales selling are developing along a similar path—because the stable, simple, and certain conditions that favored scripts have now given way to the dynamic, complex, and unpredictable conditions that favor improvisation.

Beneath the apparent chaos of improvisation is a light structure that allows it to work. Understanding that structure can help you move others, especially when your astute perspective-taking, infectious positivity, and brilliant framing don't deliver the results you seek. In those circumstances and many others, you'll do better if you follow three essential rules of improvisational theater: (1) Hear offers. (2) Say "Yes and." (3) Make your partner look good.

1. Hear offers.

Theatrical improvisation is not a complete alien on the planet of business. Scholars such as Keith Sawyer at Washington University, Mary Crossan at the University of Western Ontario, and Patricia Ryan Madson, who taught at Stanford University, have studied its dimensions and applied its concepts to management, innovation, and design.[4] But most experts haven't looked at improv in the realm of sales, even though, as one young scholar says, salespeople adept at improvising "can generate ideas, incorporate changes quickly and easily, and communicate effectively and convincingly during sales presentations."[5]

One reason for the oversight might be a legacy of a hundred-plus years of sales training. Since the days of NCR's carefully plotted scripts, salespeople have been taught to "overcome objections." If the customer doesn't want to buy, your job is to turn her around—to convince her that the problems she's raising either don't exist or don't matter. Overcoming objections is a stage in every formal sales process, one that usually follows "prospecting for leads," "qualifying leads," and "making the presentation"—and that stands just before "closing." But now that sales has changed dramatically, the very idea of turning people around might be less valuable, and perhaps less possible, than it's ever been.

Improvisational theater has no room for overcoming objections because it's built on a diametrically opposite principle. "The bread and butter of improv," says Salit, "is hearing offers."

The first principle of improvisation—hearing offers—hinges on attunement, leaving our own perspective to inhabit the perspective of another. And to master this aspect of improvisation, we must rethink our understanding of what it is to listen and what constitutes an offer.

For all the listening we do each day—by some estimates, it occupies one-fourth of our waking hours[6]—it's remarkable how profoundly we neglect this skill. As the American philosopher Mortimer Adler wrote thirty years ago:

> Is anyone anywhere taught how to listen? How utterly amazing is the general assumption that the ability to listen well is a natural gift for which no training is required. How extraordinary is the fact that no effort is made anywhere in the whole educational process to help individuals learn how to listen well.[7]

Little wonder, then, that so few of us, in fact, do listen well. For many of us, the opposite of talking isn't listening. It's waiting. When others speak, we typically divide our attention between what they're saying now and what we're going to say next—and end up doing a mediocre job at both. And a few professionals, including those who are in the business of moving others, don't even bother to wait. In one typical study, researchers found that physicians interrupt the majority of patients in the first eighteen seconds the patient speaks during an appointment, which often prevents the patient from describing what brought her to the office in the first place.[8]

That's why Salit's training emphasizes slowing down and shutting up as the route to listening well. We learn this in another exercise, called "Amazing Silence," where I'm paired with a top television executive about ten years my senior. The rules: One person has to reveal to the other something important to him. The other person, who must make eye contact the entire time, then responds—but he must wait fifteen seconds before uttering a word.

The executive opens his heart more than I expect. He tells me that after thirty-two years of demanding work, he's questioning whether what he's doing now is what he should be doing forever and whether it's time to leave the jackal-eat-jackal savannah of New York media. His eyes water a bit as he speaks, which makes me even more uncomfortable than I was doing the vertical bebop with the high-heeled cosmetics vice president.

When he's finished, I have to respond. But not yet. I begin counting down the seconds in my head. *Fifteen. Fourteen. Thirteen. No breaking eye contact. Twelve. Eleven. This is agonizing. Ten. When will the madness end?*

It does end. But those fifteen seconds feel preposterously long and, as in the earlier exercise, disturbingly intimate. And that's what Salit wants. Listening without some degree of intimacy isn't really listening. It's passive and transactional rather than active and engaged. Genuine listening is a bit like driving on a rain-slicked highway. Speed kills. If you want to get to your destination, you're better off decelerating and occasionally hitting the brake. The ultimate idea, she says, uncorking a small bottle of Zen in the cramped conference room when the session is over, is to "listen without listening *for* anything."

This is what makes improvisational theater work. Imagine a scene with two actors. The first, sitting in a chair, his hands perched on an invisible steering wheel, says to his partner, "Be sure to lock the door." The second actor hasn't been listening *for* anything. She's just been listening. Her job in that situation, Salit tells us, is to "take in anything and everything someone says as an offer you can do something with." The invisible steering wheel and the directive

"Be sure to lock the door" constitute an offer. The second actor must accept it and build on it. Maybe she's a passenger in a taxi. Maybe she's a kid in the backseat of the family car. Maybe she has a broken arm and can't reach the lock. But her ability to listen without listening *for* is what allows the scene to move forward.

Once we listen in this new, more intimate way, we begin hearing things we might have missed. And if we listen this way during our efforts to move others, we quickly realize that what seem outwardly like objections are often offers in disguise.

Take a simple example. Suppose you're raising money for a charity and you ask your brother-in-law to contribute $200. He might say no. But he's unlikely to say only that. He's more likely to say, "Sorry, I can't give two hundred dollars." That's an offer. Maybe he can donate a smaller amount. Or he might say, "No, I can't give right now." That's an offer, too. The obvious move is to fasten onto the "right now" and ask when might be a better time. But the entire sentence is an offer—perhaps to contribute to your charity some other way, say, as a volunteer. "Offers come in all shapes and sizes," says Salit. But the only way to hear them is to change the way you listen and then change the way you respond.

Which goes back to my mirroring exercise with the cosmetics executive. What each of us was doing in that session was accepting an offer. We didn't have the option of objecting. ("No way, lady, I'm not doing that with my elbow!") And once we accepted those rules, we fell into an odd but attuned ballet. Eventually, when the bell rang for us to switch roles again, our actions were so smooth that an outsider probably couldn't tell who was leading and who was following. That's the point of the first principle of improvisation. As Johnstone puts it, "Good improvisers seem telepathic; everything looks prearranged. This is because they accept all offers made."[9]

2. Say "Yes and."

The "ocean of rejection" that we face every day in sales and non-sales selling delivers plenty of nos to our shores. But we also send many back out with the tide, saying "No" ourselves more often than we realize. Improvisational theater urges actors to check this behavior—and say "Yes and" instead.

Like a potter learning to center the clay on the wheel or a tennis player acquiring the proper grip, saying "Yes and" is a foundational skill for improv artists. This second principle of improvisation depends on buoyancy, in particular the quality of positivity.

But positivity in this regard is more than avoiding no. And it's more than simply saying yes. "Yes and" carries a particular force, which becomes clearer when we contrast it with its evil twin, "Yes, but."

Nearly every improv class includes a variation on the following exercise. We didn't do this in Salit's sessions, but she showed it to me when she visited my office a few months later. The exercise involves two people who are planning a hypothetical gathering—say, a high school reunion. One person begins with a proposition—for example, "Let's have our high school reunion in Las Vegas." Every subsequent comment from both participants must begin with "Yes, but." It usually unfolds something like this:

> "Let's have our high school reunion in Las Vegas."
> "Yes, but that's going to be too expensive for some
>   people."
> "Yes, but that way only the people who really want to be
>   there will attend."

"Yes, but some of our classmates don't gamble."

"Yes, but there's more to do there than play blackjack."

"Yes, but even without gambling, it's still not a great place for people to bring their families."

"Yes, but reunions are better without all those kids."

"Yes, but if people can't find child care at home, they won't attend . . ."

The planning process spins and spins, but nothing—and nobody—moves.

Then participants take an alternative route, where the undermining conjunction "but" is replaced with its more inclusive sibling, "and." This version might go like this:

"Let's have our high school reunion in Las Vegas."

"Yes—and if it's too expensive for some people we can raise money or organize road trips."

"Yes—and if we start early, we could reserve a block of rooms at a hotel that offers volume discounts."

"Yes—and for families with kids and for people who don't gamble, we could organize activities during the day."

"Yes—and if we have enough people, we might be able to pool our resources to pay for babysitters so one night some parents can go out on their own."

"Yes—and those who wanted to could all go to a show together."

Instead of swirling downward into frustration, "Yes and" spirals upward toward possibility. When you stop you've got a set of options, not a sense of futility.

There are certainly plenty of times in life to say "No." When it comes to moving others, however, the best default position is this second principle of improv. And its benefits stretch further than sales and non-sales selling.

"'Yes and' isn't a technique," Salit says. "It's a way of life."

3. Make your partner look good.

In the summer of 2012, two giants in the field of moving others passed away. Roger Fisher, who died in August of that year shortly after reaching his ninetieth birthday, was a Harvard Law School professor and a freelance diplomatic troubleshooter. In 1981 he coauthored *Getting to Yes*, the most influential book ever written about negotiation. Fisher's signal contribution was the concept of "principled negotiation," which proposed that the aim of negotiating shouldn't be to make the other side lose but, where possible, to help it win. This idea, which quickly became shorthanded as "win-win," transformed business and legal education. Until then, many viewed negotiation as a zero-sum game, where parties vied for the largest share of a fixed pie. But Fisher's work urged young business students and law students, and less-young people inside organizations, to reframe these encounters as positive-sum games, where one person's victory didn't depend on another's defeat. If each party looks past the other party's position to its actual interests and invents options for mutual gain, negotiations could end with both sides better off than when they began.

The second giant, who died just six weeks before Fisher at the age of seventy-nine, took the core of Fisher's idea to an even larger audience. In 1989, Stephen R. Covey wrote *The 7 Habits of Highly Effective People*, which went on to sell more than twenty-five million copies. Habit 4 on Covey's list is "Think Win-Win." Establishing this habit isn't easy, he acknowledged, because "most people have been deeply scripted in the Win/Lose mentality since birth." But the only way to truly influence others is to adopt "a frame of mind and heart that constantly seeks mutual benefit in all human interactions."[10]

Because of Fisher's and Covey's influence, "win-win" has become a fixture in organizations around the world, though often more in parlance than in practice. One explanation for the disconnect between word and deed goes back to the upheaval I described in Chapter 3. Under conditions of information asymmetry, results frequently are win-lose. After all, when I know more than you, I can get what I want by beating you. And since information asymmetry was the defining condition of sales for so long, our muscle memory often takes us in that direction. But with the emergence of information parity (or at least something close to it), those instincts, developed for a different environment, can send us down the wrong path. When sellers and buyers are evenly matched, pushing for win-lose rarely leads to a win for anyone—and often ends in lose-lose.

Improv offers a way to freshen our thinking: a method that shares the worldview of Fisher and Covey but reorients it for a time when many of us have become desensitized to "win-win" from hearing it so regularly but experiencing it so rarely. In Cathy Salit and Second City's brand of theater, performers must follow this rule: Make your partner look good. Improv artists have long understood that helping your fellow performer shine helps you both create a better scene. Making your partner look good doesn't make you look worse; it actually makes you look better. It shatters the binary, either-or, zero-sum frame of mind and replaces it with a culture of generosity, creativity, and possibility. This third principle of improv—make your partner look good—calls for, and enables, clarity, the capacity to develop solutions that nobody previously imagined.

To illustrate this principle, Salit tells us to find new partners. Mine is a friendly forty-something woman who works for a large financial services company. For this exercise, called "I'm Curious," we choose a controversial issue that lends itself to opposing pro-con positions (*Should marijuana be legal? Should the death penalty be abolished?*). Then we each choose a side, with one person trying to convince the other of his or her point of view. The other person must respond, but here's the wrinkle—only with questions. The questions must be genuine queries, not veiled opinions (*Does it trouble you that the only people who share your view are imbeciles?*). They can't be yes-no questions either (*I'm right, aren't I?*). If our partner violates any of the rules—by making a statement or asking a prohibited type of question—we're to ring the motel bell to announce the violation to the whole group.

I begin in the role of questioner, and my partner stakes out a position on a long-forgotten American political controversy that happened to be front-page news the day of our seminar.

I respond to her first claim with an arch "Really?" which is technically a question but not one exactly true to the spirit of the exercise. So I gather myself and ask a real question.

She answers and expands her argument.

Trying to remember the importance of slowing down, I pause, take a breath, and begin my question with "But what about . . . ?"

A little better.

Then she moves to another line of reasoning.

Without waiting, without even realizing what I'm saying, I gasp, "You've got to be kidding!"

Ding!

Four minutes into the game, I've ended up in the penalty box.

Now it's her turn in the questioner role. Maybe because she's seen how poorly I did, she performs more nimbly. Whenever I set out an argument, her first response—every single time—is "That's so interesting!" The maneuver gives her time to conjure a question, but it also spins the weather vane in a friendlier direction. And when she poses a question, I have to stop a moment, think, and offer an intelligent answer.

The idea here isn't to win. It's to learn. And when both parties view their encounters as opportunities to learn, the desire to defeat the other side struggles to find the oxygen it needs. Questions, whose potency we've seen in both interrogative self-talk and in pitching effectively, change the rules of engagement and therefore the nature of the interaction itself. The conversation becomes more of a dance and less of a wrestling match. That's something that Fuller Brush founder Alfred Fuller intuited years before improv was ever invented. "Never argue," he wrote. "To win an argument is to lose a sale."[11]

Making your partner, the person you're selling to, look good has become even more critical than it was in Fuller's day. Back then, unscrupulous sellers didn't have to worry so much about making buyers look bad. Buyers often had nowhere else to go and nobody to tell. Today, if you make people look bad, they can tell the world. But if you make people look good, they can also tell the world.

"In improv, you never try to *get* someone to do something. That's coercion, not creativity," Salit says. "You make offers, you accept offers—and a conversation, a relationship, a scene, and other possibilities emerge."

As goes improv, so go sales and non-sales selling. If you train your ears to hear offers, if you respond to others with "Yes and," and if you always try to make your counterpart look good, possibilities will emerge.

SAMPLE CASE

•————————————•

Improvise

Take five.

Nineteen centuries ago, the Greek Stoic philosopher Epictetus said, "Nature hath given men one tongue but two ears, that we may hear from others twice as much as we speak."

Unfortunately, not many people listened to him.

You can avoid their mistake by taking Epictetus's counsel seriously. One of the simplest ways to do that—to reduce your ratio of talking to listening—is simply to slow down.

Designate one day this week to be your slow day. Then when you have a conversation, take five seconds before responding. Seriously. Every time. It will seem odd at first. And your conversation partner might wonder if you were recently bonked on the head. But pausing a few additional seconds to respond can hone your listening skills in much the same way that savoring a piece of chocolate, instead of wolfing it down, can improve your palate. (If a whole day is too much, start smaller; try it for an hour.)

Lainie Heneghan, a British consultant who advocates what she calls "radical listening," offers some ways to test whether you've slowed down enough. Are your conversation partners actually finishing their sentences? Are people getting their perspective fully on the table without your interrupting? Do they have time to take a breath before you start yapping? Taking it slower can take you further.

Say "Yes and."

One classic improv exercise is "The Ad Game." Here's how it works.

Select four or five participants. Then ask them to invent a new product and devise an advertising campaign for it. As players contribute testimonials or demonstrations or slogans, they must begin each sentence with "Yes and," which forces them to build on the previous idea. You can't refute what your colleagues say. You can't ignore it. And you shouldn't plan ahead. Just say "Yes and," accept what the person before you offers, and use it to construct an even better campaign.

"There are people who prefer to say 'Yes,' and there are people who prefer to say 'No,'" Keith Johnstone writes. "Those who say 'Yes' are rewarded by the adventures they have. Those who say 'No' are rewarded by the safety they attain."

Play "Word-at-a-time."

This is another classic improv game that has spawned lots of variations, though I like Johnstone's version best. The rules are simple. Six to eight people sit in a circle and collectively craft a story.

The hitch: Each person can add only one word and only when it's his turn.

In *Improv for Storytellers*, Johnstone describes one session with two partners helping him create. He began with the word "Sally" and what followed was this:

— Was . . .
— Going . . .
(It's my turn again, and I stir things up:) Mad . . .
— Because . . .
— Her . . .
— Father . . .
— Wanted . . .
— To . . .
— Put . . .
— His . . .
— Horse . . .
— Into . . .
— Her . . .
— Stable.

Johnstone says, "Some of these stories fizzle out after one sentence, but some may complete themselves." However the tales unfold, this exercise is great for helping you to think quickly and to tune your ears to offers.

Enlist the power of questions.

One of the Salit session exercises I enjoyed the most, "I'm Curious," is worth replicating on your own. Find a partner. Then choose a controversial issue that has two distinct and opposed sides. Before you begin, have your partner decide her position on the issue. Then you take the opposite stance. She then makes her case, but you can reply only with questions—not with statements, counterarguments, or insults.

These questions must also abide by three rules: (1) You cannot ask yes-no questions. (2) Your questions cannot be veiled opinions. (3) Your partner must answer each question.

This is tougher than it sounds. But with practice, you'll learn to use the interrogative to elevate and engage both your partner and yourself.

Read these books.

Impro: Improvisation and the Theatre by Keith Johnstone. If improvisational theater has a Lenin—a well-spoken revolutionary who provides a movement its intellectual underpinnings—that person is Johnstone. His book isn't always easy reading. It's as much a philosophical tract as the guidebook it purports to be. But it's an excellent primer for grasping the underlying principles of improvisation.

Improvisation for the Theater by Viola Spolin. If improvisational theater has an Eve—someone who was present at the creation, though in this case didn't need an Adam and didn't fall to temptation—it's Viola Spolin. This book, which came out fifty years ago, but whose updated edition remains a brisk seller, collects more than two hundred of Spolin's improv exercises.

Creating Conversations: Improvisation in Everyday Discourse by R. Keith Sawyer. Sawyer is a leading scholar of creativity. In this

2001 book, he zeroes in on our everyday conversations and shows how much these quotidian exchanges have in common with jazz, children's play, and improvisational theater. Also worth looking at is Sawyer's *Group Genius: The Creative Power of Collaboration.*

Improv Wisdom: Don't Prepare, Just Show Up by Patricia Ryan Madson. Madson, who taught drama at Stanford University until 2005, serves up thirteen maxims drawn from improv that readers can apply to their work and life.

The Second City Almanac of Improvisation by Anne Libera. One part entertainment history, another part improv guidebook, this almanac charts the rise of the Second City improv juggernaut. It's sprinkled with interesting exercises, provocative quotations on the craft, and lots of photos of well-known comedians when they were very young.

Use your thumbs.

This is a group activity that you can use to make a memorable point. Along with yourself, you'll need at least two more people as participants.

Have everyone assemble themselves into pairs. Then ask each pair to "hook the fingers of your right hands and raise your thumbs." Then, give the sole instruction: "Now get your partner's thumb down." Remain silent and allow the pairs to finish the task.

Most participants will assume that your instructions mean for them to thumb-wrestle. However, there are many other ways that they could get their partner's thumb down. They could ask nicely. They could unhook their own fingers and put their own thumb down. And so on.

The lesson here is that too often our starting point is competition—a win-lose, zero-sum approach rather than the win-win, positive-sum approach of improvisation. In most circumstances that involve moving others, we have several ways to accomplish a task, most of which can make our partners look good in the process.

9.

Serve

I f you want to travel from one town to another in Kenya, you'll probably have to step into a *matatu*, a small bus or fourteen-seat minivan that constitutes the country's main form of long-distance transportation. And if you do board one, prepare to be terrified. A young male behind the wheel of a fast-moving vehicle can be perilous in any country, but Kenyans say *matatu* drivers are especially unhinged. Like something out of *The Strange Case of Dr. Jekyll and Mr. Hyde*, otherwise kind and even-tempered Kenyan men become wild-eyed, speed-limit-crushing demons who put their passengers' lives, and their own, in danger. Partly as a consequence, Kenya has one of the highest per capita rates of traffic deaths in the world.[1]

In developing countries, road accidents now kill the same number of people as does malaria. Across the globe nearly 1.3 million people die in traffic accidents each year, making traffic injuries the world's ninth leading cause of death. The World Health Organization projects that by 2030, they will be the fifth-largest killer, ahead of HIV/AIDS, diabetes, and war and violence.[2]

Countries like Kenya call on a number of remedies for this problem. They can decrease speed limits, repair hazardous and damaged roads, encourage seat belt use, install speed bumps, and crack down on drunk driving. Many of these measures can reduce the grisly toll, but all require public money or vigilant enforcement, both of which are in short supply.

So in an ingenious field study, two Georgetown University economists, James Habyarimana and William Jack, devised a method to change the behavior of Kenya's daredevil drivers.[3] Working with the cooperatives that own the vehicles, Habyarimana and Jack recruited 2,276 *matatu* drivers. They divided everyone into two groups. Drivers with vehicles whose license plates ended in an even number became the control group. Those with an odd final digit on their license plates took part in a unique intervention. Inside each of these *matatu*s, researchers placed five stickers, in both English and Kiswahili (Kenya's national language). Some of the stickers included only words, like the ones below.*

Don't just sit there as he drives dangerously! STAND UP. SPEAK UP. NOW!

This message has been given in the interest of passenger safety with support from: OMD Colourprint

Je, ukiendeshwa vibaya, utafika? KAA MACHO. KAA CHONJO. TETA!

Huu ujumbe umeletwa kwa manufaa ya usalama wa msafiri na usaidizi kutoka: OMD   Colourp

---

*The translation of the second sign is: "Hey, if he's driving recklessly, will you arrive? BE AWAKE. BE STEADY. SPEAK UP!"

Others featured text accompanied by "explicit and gruesome images of severed body parts."[4] But all urged passengers to take action—to implore their driver to slow down, to complain loudly when he attempted breakneck maneuvers, and to browbeat him until he operated the *matatu* more like mild-mannered Dr. Jekyll than maniacal Mr. Hyde. The researchers dubbed their strategy "heckle and chide."

Over the next year, the team found that passengers riding in *matatu*s bearing stickers were three times as likely to heckle drivers as those in the stickerless *matatu*s. But did the efforts of these loud-mouthed passengers move the drivers or affect the safety of their journeys?

To find out, the researchers examined a database of claims from the insurance companies that covered the *matatu*s. The results: Total insurance claims for the vehicles with stickers fell by nearly two-thirds from the year before. Claims for serious accidents (those involving injury or death) fell by more than 50 percent. And based on follow-up interviews the researchers conducted with drivers, it was clear that the passengers' vocal persuasion efforts were the reason.[5]

In other words, adding a few stickers to the minibuses saved more money and spared more lives than just about any other effort the Kenyan government had tried. And the mechanism at work here—the stickers moved the passengers and the passengers moved the driver—offers a useful way to understand our third and final skill: to serve.

Sales and non-sales selling are ultimately about service. But "service" isn't just smiling at customers when they enter your boutique or delivering a pizza in thirty minutes or less, though both are important in the commercial realm. Instead, it's a broader, deeper, and more transcendent definition of service—improving others' lives and, in turn, improving the world. At its best, moving people can achieve something greater and more enduring than merely an exchange of resources. And that's more likely to happen if we follow the two underlying lessons of the *matatu* sticker triumph: Make it personal and make it purposeful.

Make it personal.

Radiologists lead lonely professional lives. Unlike many physicians, who spend large parts of their days interacting directly with patients, radiologists often sit alone in dimly lit rooms or hunched over computers reading X-rays, CT scans, and MRIs. Such isolation can dull these highly skilled doctors' interest in their jobs. And worse, if the work begins to feel impersonal and mechanical, it can diminish their actual performance.

A few years ago, a young Israeli radiologist named Yehonatan Turner had an inkling about how to move his fellow practitioners to do their jobs with more gusto and greater skill. Working as a resident at Shaare Zedek Medical Center in Jerusalem, Turner arranged, with patients' consent, to take photos of about three hundred people coming in for a computed tomography (CT) scan. Then he enlisted a group of radiologists, who didn't know what he was studying, for an experiment.

When the radiologists sat at their computers and called up one of these patients' CT scans to make an assessment, the patient's photograph automatically appeared next to the image. After they'd made their assessments, the radiologists completed a questionnaire. All of them reported feeling "more empathy to the patients after seeing the photograph" and being more meticulous in the way they examined the scan.[6] But the real power of Turner's idea revealed itself three months later.

One of the skills that separate outstanding radiologists from average ones is their ability to identify what are called "incidental findings," abnormalities on a scan that the physician wasn't looking for and that aren't related to the ailment for which the patient is being treated. For example, suppose I suspect that I've broken my arm and I go to the hospital for an X-ray. The doctor's main job is to see if my ulna is fractured. But if she also spots an unrelated cyst near my elbow, that's an "incidental finding." Turner selected eighty-one of the photo-accompanied scans in which his radiologists had found incidental findings and presented them again to the same group of radiologists three months later—only this time *without* the picture of the patient. (Because radiologists read so many images each day, and because they were blind to what Turner was studying, they didn't know they'd already seen these particular scans.)

The outcome was startling. Turner discovered that "80% of the incidental findings were not reported when the photograph was omitted from the file."[7] Even though the physicians were looking at precisely the same image they had scrutinized ninety days earlier, this time they were far less meticulous and far less accurate. "Our study emphasizes approaching the patient as a human being and not as an anonymous case study," Turner told *ScienceDaily.*[8]

Physicians, like all the rest of us, are in the moving business. But in order for them to do their jobs well—that is, to move people from sickness and injury to health and well-being—doctors fare better when they make it personal. Instead of seeing patients as duffel bags of symptoms, viewing them as full-fledged human beings helps physicians in their work and patients in their treatment. This doesn't mean doctors and nurses should abandon checklists and protocols.[9] But it does mean that a single-minded reliance on processes and algorithms that obscure the human being on the other side of the transaction is akin to a clinical error. As Turner's study shows—and because of his work, photographs are now being added to Pap smear specimens, blood tests, and other diagnostics[10]—injecting the personal into the professional can boost performance and increase quality of care.

And what's true for doctors is true for the rest of us. Every circumstance in which we try to move others by definition involves another human being. Yet in the name of professionalism, we often neglect the human element and adopt a stance that's abstract and distant. Instead, we should recalibrate our approach so that it's concrete and personal—and not for softhearted reasons but for hardheaded ones. The general problem of road safety in Kenya is abstract and distant. Equipping individual passengers to influence their very own *matatu* driver while he is driving them makes it concrete and personal. Reading a CT scan alone in a room is abstract and distant. Reading a CT scan when a photograph of the patient is staring back at you makes it concrete and personal. In both traditional sales and non-sales selling, we do better when we move beyond solving a puzzle to serving a person.

But the value of making it personal has two sides. One is recognizing the person you're trying to serve, as in remembering the individual human being behind the CT scan. The other is putting yourself personally behind whatever it is that you're trying to sell. I've seen this flip side in action not in the pages of a social science journal or the corridors of a radiology lab, but on the walls of a pizzeria in Washington, D.C.

One Saturday night last year, my wife and two of our three kids decided to try a new restaurant, Il Canale, an inexpensive Italian place that had been recommended by friends from Italy. We had to wait a few minutes before being seated. And since I suffer from inveterate pacing disorder, I did a few laps inside the small front lobby. But I halted when I saw this framed sign with a photograph of the restaurant's owner, Giuseppe Farruggio:

I need your help!
If you had anything less than a
great experience at *il Canale*
please call my cell. 703-624-2111

Farruggio, who came to the United States from Sicily when he was seventeen, is in sales, of course. He's selling fresh antipasti, linguine alle vongole, and certified Neapolitan pizza to hungry families. But with this sign, he's transforming his offering from distant and abstract—Washington, D.C., is not short on places that serve pizza and pasta—to concrete and personal. And he's doing it in an especially audacious way. For Farruggio, service isn't about delivering a calzone in twenty-nine minutes. For him, service is about literally being at the call of his customers.

When I talked with him a few weeks later about the response he'd gotten, Farruggio said that in the first eighteen months he posted the sign, he received a total of only eight calls. Six were from people offering praise—or perhaps testing if the promise was for real. Two came from customers with complaints, which Farruggio used to improve his service. (Dear reader, please do not call Mr. Farruggio's mobile phone unless you have a bad meal at Il Canale, which in my experience occurs roughly never.) But the importance of what he's doing isn't the calls he's receiving from customers. It's what he's communicating to them—namely, that there's a person behind the pizza and that person cares about whether his guests are happy. Just as putting a photograph alongside the CT scan changes the way radiologists do their jobs, putting his own smiling face and phone number above the front cash register changes the way customers experience Farruggio's restaurant. Many of us like to say, "I'm accountable" or "I care." Few of us are so deeply committed to serving others that we're willing to say, "Call my cell."

Farruggio's style of making it personal is characteristic of many of the most successful sellers. Brett Bohl, who runs Scrubadoo .com, which sells medical scrubs, sends a handwritten note to every single customer who buys one of his products.[11] Tammy Darvish, the car dealer we met in Chapter 3, gives her home e-mail address to all of her customers, telling them, "If you have any questions or concerns, contact me personally." They do. And when she responds, they know she's there to serve.

Make it purposeful.

American hospitals aren't as dangerous as Kenyan *matatu*s, but they're far less safe than you'd think. Each year, about 1 out of every 20 hospitalized patients contracts an infection in a U.S. hospital and the resulting toll is staggering: ninety-nine thousand annual deaths and a yearly cost of upward of $40 billion.[12] The most cost-effective way to prevent these infections is for doctors, nurses, and other health care professionals to regularly wash their hands. But the frequency of hand washing in U.S. hospitals is astonishingly low. And many of the efforts to get more people scrubbing their hands more often have been sadly ineffective.

Adam Grant, the Wharton professor whose research on ambiversion I discussed in Chapter 4, decided to see if he could find a better way to move those working inside hospitals to change their behavior. In research he conducted with David Hofmann of the University of North Carolina, Grant tried out three different approaches to this non-sales selling challenge. The two researchers went to a U.S. hospital and obtained permission to post signs next to sixty-six of the hospital's soap and hand-sanitizing gel dispensers for two weeks. One-third of those signs appealed to the health care professionals' self-interest:

HAND HYGIENE PREVENTS YOU
FROM CATCHING DISEASES.

One-third emphasized the consequences for patients, that is, the purpose of the hospital's work:

HAND HYGIENE PREVENTS PATIENTS
FROM CATCHING DISEASES.

The final one-third of the signs included a snappy slogan and served as the control condition:

GEL IN, WASH OUT.

The researchers weighed the bags of soap and gel at the beginning of the two-week period and weighed them again at the end to see how much the employees actually used. And when they tabulated the results, they found that the most effective sign, by far, was the second one. "The amount of hand-hygiene product used from dispensers with the patient-consequences sign was significantly greater than the amount used from dispensers with the personal-consequences sign . . . or the control sign," Grant and Hofmann wrote.[13]

Intrigued by the results, the researchers decided to test the robustness of their findings nine months later in different units of the same hospital. This time they used only two signs—the personal-consequences version (HAND HYGIENE PREVENTS YOU FROM CATCHING DISEASES) and the patient-consequences one (HAND HYGIENE PREVENTS PATIENTS FROM CATCHING DISEASES). And instead of weighing bags of soap and sanitizer, they recruited hospital personnel to be their hand-washing spies. Over a two-week period, these recruits, who weren't told the nature of the study, covertly recorded when doctors, nurses, and other health care staff faced a "hand-hygiene opportunity" and whether these employees actually hygiened their hands when the opportunity arose. Once again, the personal-consequences sign had zero effect. But the sign appealing to purpose boosted hand washing by 10 percent overall and significantly more for the physicians.[14]

Clever signs alone won't eliminate hospital-acquired infections. As surgeon Atul Gawande has observed, checklists and other processes can be highly effective on this front.[15] But Grant and Hofmann reveal something equally crucial: "Our findings suggest that health and safety messages should focus not on the self, but rather on the target group that is perceived as most vulnerable."[16]

Raising the salience of purpose is one of the most potent—and most overlooked—methods of moving others. While we often assume that human beings are motivated mainly by self-interest, a stack of research has shown that all of us also do things for what social scientists call "prosocial" or "self-transcending" reasons.[17] That means that not only should we ourselves be serving, but we should also be tapping others' innate desire to serve. Making it personal works better when we also make it purposeful.

To take just one example from the research, a team of British and New Zealand scholars recently conducted a pair of clever experiments in another non-sales selling context. They randomly assigned their participants to three groups. One group read information about why car-sharing is good for the environment. (Researchers dubbed these folks the "self-transcending group.") One read about why car-sharing can save people money. (This was the "self-interested group.") The third, the control group, read general information about car travel. Then the participants filled out a few unrelated questionnaires to occupy their time. When they were done, they were dismissed and told to discard any remaining papers they still had. And to do that, they had two choices—a clearly marked bin for regular waste and a clearly marked bin for recycling. About half of the people in the second and third groups—the "self-interested" and control groups—recycled their papers. But in the "self-transcending" first group, nearly 90 percent chose to recycle.[18] Merely discussing purpose in one realm (car-sharing) moved people to behave differently in a second realm (recycling).

What's more, Grant's research has shown that purpose is a performance enhancer not only in efforts like the promotion of hand washing and recycling, but also in traditional sales. In 2008, he carried out a fascinating study of a call center at a major U.S. university. Each night, employees made phone calls to alumni to raise money for the school. As is the habit of social psychologists, Grant randomly organized the fund-raisers into three groups. Then he arranged their work conditions to be identical—except for the five minutes prior to their shift.

For two consecutive nights, one group read stories from people who'd previously worked in the call center, explaining that the job had taught them useful sales skills (perhaps attunement, buoyancy, and clarity). This was the "personal benefit group." Another—the "purpose group"—read stories from university alumni who'd received scholarships funded by the money this call center had raised describing how those scholarships had helped them. The third collection of callers was the control group, who read stories that had nothing to do with either personal benefit or purpose. After the reading exercise, the workers hit the phones, admonished not to mention the stories they'd just read to the people they were trying to persuade to donate money.

A few weeks later, Grant looked at their sales numbers. The "personal benefit" and control groups secured about the same number of pledges and raised about the same amount of money as they had in the period before the story-reading exercise. But the people in the purpose group kicked into overdrive. They more than doubled "the number of weekly pledges that they earned and the amount of weekly donation money that they raised."[19]

Sales trainers, take note. This five-minute reading exercise more than *doubled* production. The stories made the work personal; their contents made it purposeful. This is what it means to serve: improving another's life and, in turn, improving the world. That's the lifeblood of service and the final secret to moving others.

In 1970, an obscure sixty-six-year-old former mid-level AT&T executive named Robert Greenleaf wrote an essay that launched a movement. He titled it "Servant as Leader"—and in a few dozen earnest pages, he turned the reigning philosophies of business and political leadership upside down. Greenleaf argued that the most effective leaders weren't heroic, take-charge commanders but instead were quieter, humbler types whose animating purpose was to serve those nominally beneath them. Greenleaf called his notion "servant leadership" and explained that the order of those two words held the key to its meaning. "The servant-leader is servant first," he wrote. "Becoming a servant-leader begins with the natural feeling that one wants to serve, to serve first. Then conscious choice brings one to aspire to lead."[20]

The very idea of leaders subordinating themselves to followers, of inverting the traditional pyramid, made many people uncomfortable. But Greenleaf's philosophy excited many more. Those who embraced it learned to "do no harm," to respond "to any problem by listening first," and to "accept and empathize" rather than reject. Over time, companies as diverse as Starbucks, TD Industries, Southwest Airlines, and Brooks Brothers integrated Greenleaf's ideas into their management practices. Business schools added Greenleaf to their reading lists and syllabi. Nonprofit organizations and religious institutions introduced his principles to their members.

What helped servant leadership take hold wasn't merely that many of those who tried it found it effective. It was also that the approach gave voice to their latent beliefs about other people and their deeper aspirations for themselves. Greenleaf's way of leading was more difficult, but it was also more transformative. As he wrote, "The best test, and the most difficult to administer, is this: Do those served grow as persons? Do they, while being served, become healthier, wiser, freer, more autonomous, more likely themselves to become servants?"[21]

The time is ripe for the sales version of Greenleaf's philosophy. Call it servant selling. It begins with the idea that those who move others aren't manipulators but servants. They serve first and sell later. And the test—which, like Greenleaf's, is the best and the most difficult to administer—is this: If the person you're selling to agrees to buy, will his or her life improve? When your interaction is over, will the world be a better place than when you began?

Servant selling is the essence of moving others today. But in some sense, it has always been present in those who've granted sales its proper respect. For instance, Alfred Fuller, the man whose company gave Norman Hall his unlikely vocation, said that at a critical point in his own career, he realized that his work was better— in all senses of the word—when he served first and sold next. He began thinking of himself as a civic reformer, a benefactor to families, and "a crusader against unsanitary kitchens and inadequately cleaned homes." It seemed a bit silly, he admitted. "But the successful seller must feel some commitment that his product offers mankind as much altruistic benefit as it yields the seller in money." An effective seller isn't a "huckster, who is just out for profit," he said. The true "salesman is an idealist and an artist."[22]

So, too, is the true person. Among the things that distinguish our species from others is our combination of idealism and artistry—our desire both to improve the world and to provide that world with something it didn't know it was missing. Moving others doesn't require that we neglect these nobler aspects of our nature. Today it demands that we embrace them. It begins and ends by remembering that to sell is human.

SAMPLE CASE

Serve

Move from "upselling" to "upserving."

One of the most detestable words in the lexicon of sales is "upselling." You go to the sporting goods store for basic running shoes and the salesperson tries to get you to buy the priciest pair on the shelf. You purchase a camera and the guy behind the counter presses you to buy a kit that's no good, accessories you don't want, and an extended warranty you don't need. Once, when ordering something online, before I was able to check out, the site pelted me with about half a dozen add-ons in which I had no interest—and when I looked at the Web address, it read http://www.nameofthecompany.com/upsell. (I quit the transaction there—and never bought anything from that operation again.)

Sadly, many traditional sales training programs still teach people to upsell. But if they were smarter, they'd banish both the concept and the word—and replace it with a far friendlier, and demonstrably more effective, alternative.

Upserve.

Upserving means doing more for the other person than he expects or you initially intended, taking the extra steps that transform a mundane interaction into a memorable experience. This simple move—from upselling to upserving—has the obvious advantage of being the right thing to do. But it also carries the hidden advantage of being extraordinarily effective.

Anytime you're tempted to upsell someone else, stop what you're doing and upserve instead. Don't try to increase what they can do for you. Elevate what you can do for them.

Rethink sales commissions.

Even after reading this book, you might still believe that traditional salespeople just aren't like the rest of us. You and I have a mix of motives, many of them high-minded—but not those folks who sell household appliances or home security systems. They're different. They are—and here's an adjective I hear a lot—"coin-operated." (Slip a quarter in their slot and they'll do a little dance. When time runs out, insert another coin or they'll stop dancing!) That's why we usually rely on sales commissions to motivate and compensate people in traditional sales. It's the best—perhaps the only—way to get them to move.

But what if we're wrong? What if we offer commissions largely because, well, we've always offered commissions? What if the practice has so cemented into orthodoxy that it's ceased being an actual decision? And what if it actually stands in the way of the ability to serve?

That's what Microchip Technology, a $6.5 billion American

semiconductor company, suspected. It once paid its sales force in accordance with the industry standard—60 percent base salary, 40 percent commissions. But thirteen years ago, Microchip abolished that scheme and replaced it with a package of 90 percent base salary and 10 percent variable compensation tied to company growth. What happened? Total sales increased. The cost of sales stayed the same. Attrition dropped. And Microchip has rung up profits every quarter since—in one of the most brutally competitive industries around.

From giant multinationals like GlaxoSmithKline to small insurance companies in Oregon to software start-ups in Cambridge, England, many companies are questioning this long-established practice, implementing new strategies, and seeing great results. They're finding that paying their sales force in other ways has many virtues. It eliminates the problem of people gaming the system for their own advantage. It promotes collaboration. (If I get paid only for what I sell, why should I help you?) It spares managers the time and burden of resolving endless compensation disputes. Most of all, it can make salespeople the agents of their customers rather than their adversaries, removing a barrier to serving them thoroughly and authentically.

Should every company forsake sales commissions? No. But simply challenging the orthodoxy can be healthy. As Microchip's vice president of sales told me: "Salespeople are no different from engineers, architects, or accountants. Really good salespeople want to solve problems and serve customers. They want to be part of something larger than themselves."

Recalibrate your notion
of who's doing whom a favor.

Seth Godin, the marketing guru and one of the most creative people I know, has a great way of explaining how we categorize our sales and non-sales selling transactions. We divide them, he says, into three categories.

We think, "I'm doing you a favor, bud." Or "Hey, this guy is doing me a favor." Or "This is a favorless transaction."

Problems arise, Godin says, "when one party in the transaction thinks he's doing the other guy a favor . . . but the other guy doesn't act that way in return."

The remedy for this is simple and it's one we can use in our efforts to move others: "Why not always act as if the other guy is doing the favor?"

This approach connects to the quality of attunement—in particular, the finding that lowering your status can enhance your powers of perspective-taking. And it demonstrates that as with servant leadership, the wisest and most ethical way to move others is to proceed with humility and gratitude.

Try "emotionally intelligent signage."

You probably noticed that many examples in this chapter—from the Kenyan *matatu*s to Il Canale's pizzeria—involved signs. Signs are an integral part of our visual environment, but we often don't employ them with sufficient sophistication.

One way to do better is with what I call "emotionally intelligent signage." Most signs typically have two functions: They

provide information to help people find their way or they announce rules. But emotionally intelligent signage goes deeper. It
achieves those same ends by enlisting the principles of "make it
personal" and "make it purposeful." It tries to move others by
expressing empathy with the person viewing the sign (that's the
personal part) or by triggering empathy in that person so she'll
understand the rationale behind the posted rule (that's the purposeful part).

Here's an example of the first variety. A few years ago, my family and I were visiting a museum in New York City. Shortly after
we arrived, several of the smaller family members reported feeling
hungry, which forced us to spend some of our limited time roam-
ing a cafeteria looking for pudding rather than walking the museum looking at pictures. When we arrived at the eatery, the line
to get food curled around a corner like an anaconda. I grimaced,
thinking we'd be there forever. But moments after unscrunching
my face, I saw this sign:

My cortisol level dropped. The line turned out not to be nearly as long as I feared. And I spent my short wait in a better mood. By empathizing with line-waiters—making it personal—the sign transformed the experience of being in that space.

For an example of the second variety of emotionally intelligent signs, I simply visited a neighborhood near my own in Washington, D.C. On one busy corner is a small church that sits on an enormous lawn. Many people in the area walk their dogs. And the combination of lots of dogs and a giant expanse of grass can lead to an obvious (and odorous) problem. To avert that problem, that is, to move dog-walkers to change their behavior, the church could have posted a sign that merely announced its rules. Something like this, for instance, which I've doctored a bit from the original:

However, the church took a different approach and posted the following sign instead:

By reminding people of the reason for the rule and trying to trigger empathy on the part of those dog-walkers—making it purposeful—the sign-makers increased the likelihood that people would behave as the sign directed.

Now your assignment: Take one of the signs you now use or see in your workplace or community and recast it so it's more emotionally intelligent. By making it personal, or making it purposeful, you'll make it better.

Treat everybody as you would your grandmother.

Yehonatan Turner, the Israeli radiologist who led the photo study, told *The New York Times* that the way he first dealt with the impersonal nature of his job was to imagine that every scan he looked at was his father's.

You can borrow from his insight with this simple technique for moving others. In every encounter, imagine that the person you're dealing with is your grandmother. This is the ultimate way to make it personal. How would you behave if the person walking into your car lot wasn't a stranger but instead was Grandma? What changes would you make if the employee you're about to ask to take on an unpleasant assignment wasn't a seemingly disposable new hire but was the woman who gave birth to one of your parents? How honest and ethical would you be if the person you're corresponding with via e-mail wasn't a onetime collaborator but was the nice lady who still sends you birthday cards with a $5 bill tucked inside?

By removing the cloak of anonymity and replacing it with this form of personal connection, you're more likely to genuinely serve, which over the long haul will redound to everyone's benefit.

And if you're skeptical, try this variation. Treat everyone as you'd treat your grandmother, but assume that Grandma has eighty thousand Twitter followers.

Always ask—and answer—these two questions.

Finally, at every opportunity you have to move someone—from traditional sales, like convincing a prospect to buy a new computer system, to non-sales selling, like persuading your daughter to do her homework—be sure you can answer the two questions at the core of genuine service.

1. If the person you're selling to agrees to buy, will his or her life improve?

2. When your interaction is over, will the world be a
   better place than when you began?

If the answer to either of these questions is no, you're doing
something wrong.

Acknowledgments

To sell may be human. To write a book, not so much—at least not the lumbering and painful way I do it.

That's why I'm grateful I had so many people in my corner.

Rafe Sagalyn, the world's best literary agent, recognized the possibilities of this book well before its author did. His counsel and his friendship mean the world to me. Thanks also to Lauren Clark for taking care of business on the international front.

At Riverhead Books, Jake Morrissey was, as always, smart and unflappable—particularly when people like me were being not so smart and flapping wildly. Geoff Kloske put his considerable editorial acumen and publishing muscle behind this project, for which I'm grateful. And a ginormous thanks to Riverhead's production department for its heroic efforts when I sent the game into overtime.

Elizabeth McCullough assisted in ways large and small—from excavating obscure studies in the University of Virginia Library to discovering typos everybody else missed to schooling me on endnote formatting. Cindy Huggett, one of America's best training and development minds, was masterful in helping me make the Sample Cases useful and coherent. Rob Ten Pas once again contributed several fine illustrations.

The fabulous Pink kids—Sophia, Eliza, and Saul—calmly endured their dad's writing another book. (Alas, convincing them of the awesomeness of the resulting denied vacations, hurried meals, and missed baseball games proved to be a hard sell.)

But the most important person, in this and in all things, was Jessica Lerner. Jessica read every word of this book. Several times. Out loud. If that wasn't enough, she also listened to me read each page. Several times. Out loud. She proofed, prodded, and pushed back—and did it all with the same astonishing combination of brainpower and tenderness she brings to everything she does. I didn't know it at the time, but the smartest pitch I ever made occurred twenty-two years ago when I persuaded her to go out on a date with me. I've been sold ever since.

Notes

CHAPTER 1. WE'RE ALL IN SALES NOW

1. Alfred C. Fuller (as told to Hartzell Spence), *A Foot in the Door: The Life Appraisal of the Original Fuller Brush Man* (New York: McGraw-Hill, 1960), 2.
2. John Bainbridge, "May I Just Step Inside?" *The New Yorker*, November 13, 1948.
3. "The Ups and Downs of the Fuller Brush Co.," *Fortune,* 1938, available at http://features.blogs.fortune.cnn.com/2012/02/26/the-fuller-brush-co-fortune-1938/; Gerald Carson, "The Fuller Brush Man," *American Heritage*, August–September 1986; Bainbridge, "May I Just Step Inside?"
4. Carson, "The Fuller Brush Man."
5. Fuller, *A Foot in the Door,* 197–98.
6. See, for instance, James Ledbetter, "Death of a Salesman. Of Lots of Them, Actually," *Slate*, September 21, 2010. Available at http://www.slate.com/articles/business/moneybox/2010/09/death_of_a_salesman_of_lots_of_them_actually.html.
7. U.S. Bureau of Labor Statistics, "Occupational Employment and Wages Summary (2011)," released March 27, 2012. See Table 1, which is available at http://www.bls.gov/news.release/ocwage.t01.htm. The OES data show 13.65 million people in "Sales and Related Occupations" and another 328,000 "Sales Managers." However, the OES survey does not include "the self-employed, or owners in partners in unincorporated firms." If we make the conservative assumption that just 1 in 10 of these roughly fourteen million workers are in sales, too, that puts the total figure over fifteen million, which represents about 11 percent of the entire workforce. See "Occupational Employment and Wages Technical Note," available at http://www.bls.gov/news.release/ocwage.tn.htm. See also U.S. Census Bureau, *The Statistical Abstract of the United States: 2012,* 131st ed., Table 606, which suggests that more than 16 percent of the self-employed are in "sales and office occupations." The labor economics consulting firm Economic Modeling Specialists Intl. likewise argues that one reason for the seeming drop in the number of salespeople is that huge numbers have gone from traditional

employment to independent contractor status: "Sales jobs (like other jobs) are not disappearing from the economy nearly as much as they are disappearing as traditional, 'covered' employment—all the while, growing in numbers and size outside the spotlight of the usual employment datasets." EMSI's analysis is available at http://www.economicmodeling.com/2010/09/30/the-premature -death-of-the-salesman/.

8. U.S. Census Bureau, *The Statistical Abstract of the United States: 2012,* 131st ed. See page 300, Tables 461 and 462 and page 18, Table 13. One technical note: Government jobs and manufacturing jobs—that is, jobs grouped by sector—are tabulated monthly in the *Employment Situation* report. Sales jobs, as noted above, are tabulated twice a year in the Occupational Employment and Wages Summary, which groups jobs by occupation.

9. C. Brett Lockard and Michael Wolf, "Occupational Employment Projections to 2020," *Monthly Labor Review* 135, no. 1 (January 2012): 84–108. See page 88 and Table 1.

10. Statistics Canada, *Monthly Labour Force Survey*, "Average Hourly Wages of Employees by Selected Characteristic and Profession," April 2012, available at http://www.statcan.gc.ca/tables-tableaux/sum-som/l01/cst01/labr69a-eng.htm; Australian Bureau of Statistics, *2006 Census Tables*, Table 20680, available at http://www.censusdata.abs.gov.au/; Office for (UK) National Statistics, "Labour Force Survey Employment Status by Occupation, April–June 2011," available at http://www.ons.gov.uk/ons/publications/re-reference-tables.html?edition =tcm:77-215723.

11. The total number of employed persons in the EU is roughly 216 million. The total number of people employed in sales functions is roughly 29 million. Monika Wozowczyk and Nicola Massarelli, "European Union Labour Force Survey—Annual Results 2010," *Eurostat Statistics in Focus*, June 23, 2011; Vincent Bourgeais, Eurostat Media and Institutional Support, correspondence with author, May 17–22, 2012.

12. Japanese Ministry of Internal Affairs and Communications Statistics Bureau, *The Statistical Handbook of Japan 2011*, Table 12.3, "Employment by Occupation," available in English at http://www.stat.go.jp/english/data/handbook/c12cont. htm#cha12_1.

13. China has 36.7 percent of its workforce in agriculture, and India 18.1 percent, according to *The CIA World Factbook (2012)*, available at http://1.usa.gov/2J7bUe and http://1.usa.gov/9doDpD.

14. Adi Narayan, "Welcome to India, the Land of the Drug Reps," *Bloomberg BusinessWeek*, September 8, 2011.

15. See "How Does Gallup Polling Work?" available at http://www.gallup.com/ poll/101872/how-does-gallup-polling-work.aspx.

CHAPTER 2. ENTREPRENEURSHIP, ELASTICITY, AND ED-MED

1. U.S. Census Bureau, 2009, "Nonemployer Statistics," available at http://www .census.gov/econ/nonemployer.

2. Kaomi Goetz, "For Freelancers, Landing a Workspace Gets Harder," NPR, April 10, 2012, available at http://www.npr.org/2012/04/10/150286116/for-freelancers-landing-a-workspace-gets-harder.

3. Ryan Kim, "By 2020, Independent Workers Will Be a Majority," *GigaOm*, December 8, 2011, available at http://gigaom.com/2011/12/08/mbo-partners-network-2011/; Kauffman Foundation, "Young Invincibles Policy Brief: New Poll Finds More Than Half of Millennials Want to Start Businesses," November 10, 2011, available at http://www.kauffman.org/uploadedfiles/millennials_study.pdf.

4. OECD (2011), *Entrepreneurship at a Glance 2011,* OECD Publishing. Available at http://dx.doi.org/10.1787/9789264097711-en; Donna J. Kelley, Slavica Singer, and Mike Herrington, *Global Entrepreneurship Monitor 2011 Global Report* (2012), 12. Available at http://gemconsortium.org/docs/2409/gem-2011-global-report.

5. Adam Davidson, "Don't Mock the Artisanal-Pickle-Makers," *New York Times Magazine*, February 15, 2012.

6. "The Return of Artisanal Employment," *Economist*, October 31, 2011. A handful of you might remember that I made a similar argument a decade ago in Daniel H. Pink, *Free Agent Nation: The Future of Working for Yourself* (New York: Business Plus, 2002).

7. The latest Etsy data are available at http://www.etsy.com/press.

8. Robert Atkinson, "It's the Digital Economy, Stupid," *Fast Company,* January 8, 2009.

9. Carl Franzen, "Kickstarter Expects to Provide More Funding to the Arts Than NEA," *Talking Points Memo*, February 24, 2012, available at http://idealab.talkingpointsmemo.com/2012/02/kickstarter-expects-to-provide-more-funding-to-the-arts-than-nea.php; Carl Franzen, "NEA Weighs In on Kickstarter Funding Debate," *Talking Points Memo*, February 27, 2012, available at http://idealab.talkingpointsmemo.com/2012/02/the-nea-responds-to-kickstarter-funding-debate.php. That said, Kickstarter has a high failure rate. Roughly half the projects that seek funding don't succeed in reaching their target. See Samantha Murphy, "About 41% of Kickstarter Projects Fail," *Mashable Tech*, June 12, 2012, available at http://mashable.com/2012/06/12/kickstarter-failures/.

10. Comments at Wired Business Conference, New York City, May 1, 2012.

11. Michael Mandel, "Where the Jobs Are: The App Economy," TechNet white paper, February 7, 2012, available at http://www.technet.org/wp-content/uploads/2012/02/TechNet-App-Economy-Jobs-Study.pdf.

12. Michael DeGusta, "Are Smart Phones Spreading Faster Than Any Technology in Human History?" *Technology Review*, May 9, 2012.

13. "Cisco Visual Networking Index: Global Mobile Data Traffic Forecast Update, 2011–2016," February 14, 2012, available at http://www.cisco.com/en/US/solutions/collateral/ns341/ns525/ns537/ns705/ns827/white_paper_c11-520862.pdf.

14. Dominic Basulto, "10 Billion Tiny Screens Can Change the World," *Big Think*, February 22, 2012, available at http://bigthink.com/endless-innovation/10-billion-tiny-screens-can-change-the-world.

15. U.S. Bureau of Labor Statistics, *Occupational Outlook Handbook*, March 29, 2012,

available at http://www.bls.gov/ooh/home.htm. See also Anthony P. Carnevale, Nicole Smith, Artem Gulish, and Bennett H. Beach, "Healthcare," a report by the Georgetown University Center on Education and the Workforce (June 21, 2012), which projects between a 25 and 31 percent increase in health care jobs in the United States by 2020; available at http://www.healthreformgps.org/wp-content/uploads/Healthcare.FullReport.071812.pdf.

16. "Friday Thoughts," *White Coat Underground*, June 24, 2011, available at http://whitecoatunderground.com/2011/06/24/friday-thoughts/.

17. Rosabeth Moss Kanter, "The 'White Coat' Economy of Massachusetts," *Boston Globe*, May 9, 2006; Derek Thompson, "America 2020: Health Care Nation," *Atlantic*, August 17, 2010, available at http://www.theatlantic.com/business/archive/2010/08/america-2020-health-care-nation/61647/.

CHAPTER 3. FROM *CAVEAT EMPTOR* TO *CAVEAT VENDITOR*

1. George A. Akerlof, "Writing 'The Market for "Lemons"'": A Personal and Interpretive Essay," available at http://www.nobelprize.org/nobel_prizes/economics/laureates/2001/akerlof-article.html.

2. George A. Akerlof, "The Market for 'Lemons': Quality Uncertainty and the Market Mechanism," *Quarterly Journal of Economics* 84, no. 3 (August 1970): 488–500.

3. Ibid., 489.

4. Joe Girard with Stanley H. Brown, *How to Sell Anything to Anybody* (New York: Fireside, 2006; 1977), 6.

5. Ibid., 251.

6. Ibid., 121, 173.

7. Ibid., 49–51.

8. Ibid., 53.

9. Doug Gross, "Are Social Media Making the Resume Obsolete?" CNN.com, July 11, 2012, available at http://www.cnn.com/2012/07/11/tech/social-media/facebook-jobs-resume/index.html.

10. Fortune 500, 2012 list, available at http://money.cnn.com/magazines/fortune/fortune500/2012/full_list/.

11. Alfred C. Fuller (as told to Hartzell Spence), *A Foot in the Door: The Life Appraisal of the Original Fuller Brush Man* (New York: McGraw-Hill, 1960), xx.

12. See, for instance, John F. Tanner Jr., George W. Dudley, and Lawrence B. Chonko, "Salesperson Motivation and Success: Examining the Relationship Between Motivation and Sales Approach," paper presented at annual convention of the Society for Marketing Advances, San Antonio, Texas (November 2005).

CHAPTER 4. ATTUNEMENT

1. Adam D. Galinsky, Joe C. Magee, M. Ena Inesi, and Deborah H. Gruenfeld, "Power and Perspectives Not Taken," *Psychological Science* 17 (December 2006): 1068–74.

2. Ibid., 1070.

3. Ibid., 1071.

4. Britt Peterson, "Why It Matters That Our Politicians Are Rich," *Boston Globe*, February 19, 2012. See also Michael W. Kraus, Paul K. Piff, and Dacher Keltner, "Social Class as Culture: The Convergence of Resources and Rank in the Social Realm," *Current Directions in Psychological Science* 20, no. 4 (August 2011): 246–50.

5. Adam D. Galinsky, William W. Maddux, Debra Gilin, and Judith B. White, "Why It Pays to Get Inside the Head of Your Opponent: The Differential Effects of Perspective Taking and Empathy in Negotiations," *Psychological Science* 19, no. 4 (April 2008): 378–84.

6. Pauline W. Chen, "Can Doctors Learn Empathy?" *New York Times*, June 21, 2012.

7. Galinsky et al., "Why It Pays," 383.

8. For a good and accessible introduction to the field of social network analysis, see the work of Valdis Krebs, available at http://www.orgnet.com. An excellent introductory book on the topic is Lee Rainie and Barry Wellman, *Networked: The New Social Operating System* (Cambridge, MA: MIT Press, 2012).

9. William W. Maddux, Elizabeth Mullen, and Adam D. Galinsky, "Chameleons Bake Bigger Pies and Take Bigger Pieces: Strategic Behavioral Mimicry Facilitates Negotiation Outcomes," *Journal of Experimental Social Psychology* 44, no. 2 (March 2008): 461–68.

10. "The chameleon effect refers to nonconscious mimicry of the postures, mannerisms, facial expressions, and other behaviors of one's interaction partners, such that one's behavior passively and unintentionally changes to match that of others in one's current social environment." Tanya L. Chartrand and John A. Bargh, "The Chameleon Effect: The Perception-Behavior Link and Social Interaction," *Journal of Personality and Social Psychology* 76, no. 6 (June 1999): 893–910.

11. Maddux et al., "Chameleons Bake Bigger Pies," 463.

12. Ibid., 466.

13. Ibid., 461.

14. Adrienne Murrill, "Imitation Is Best Form of Flattery—and a Good Negotiation Strategy," *Kellogg News*, August 16, 2007. Available at http://www.kellogg.northwestern.edu/news_articles/2007/aom-mimicry.aspx.

15. Rick B. van Baaren, Rob W. Holland, Bregje Steenaert, and Ad van Knippenberg, "Mimicry for Money: Behavioral Consequences of Imitation," *Journal of Experimental Social Psychology* 39, no. 4 (July 2003): 393–98.

16. Céline Jacob, Nicolas Guéguen, Angélique Martin, and Gaëlle Boulbry, "Retail Salespeople's Mimicry of Customers: Effects on Consumer Behavior," *Journal of Retailing and Consumer Services* 18, no. 5 (September 2011): 381–88.

17. Robin J. Tanner, Rosellina Ferraro, Tanya L. Chartrand, James R. Bettman, and Rick Van Baaren, "Of Chameleons and Consumption: The Impact of Mimicry on Choice and Preferences," *Journal of Consumer Research* 34 (April 2008): 754–66.

18. April H. Crusco and Christopher G. Wetzel, "The Midas Touch: The Effects of Interpersonal Touch on Restaurant Tipping," *Personality and Social Psychology Bulletin* 10, no. 4 (December 1984): 512–17; Céline Jacob and Nicolas Guéguen,

"The Effect of Physical Distance Between Patrons and Servers on Tipping," *Journal of Hospitality & Tourism Research* 36, no. 1 (February 2012): 25–31.

19. Nicolas Guéguen, "Courtship Compliance: The Effect of Touch on Women's Behavior," *Social Influence* 2, no. 2 (2007): 81–97.

20. Frank N. Willis and Helen K. Hamm, "The Use of Interpersonal Touch in Securing Compliance," *Journal of Nonverbal Behavior* 5, no. 5 (September 1980): 49–55.

21. Damien Erceau and Nicolas Guéguen, "Tactile Contact and Evaluation of the Toucher," *Journal of Social Psychology* 147, no. 4 (August 2007): 441–44.

22. See also Liam C. Kavanagh, Christopher L. Suhler, Patricia S. Churchland, and Piotr Winkielman, "When It's an Error to Mirror: The Surprising Reputational Costs of Mimicry," *Psychological Science* 22, no. 10 (October 2011): 1274–76.

23. Daniel Kahneman, Ed Diener, and Norbert Schwarz, eds., *Well-Being: The Foundations of Hedonic Psychology* (New York: Russell Sage Foundation, 1999), 218.

24. P. T. Costa Jr. and R. R. McCrae, *NEO PI-R Professional Manual* (Odessa, FL: Psychological Assessment Resources, Inc., 1992), 15; Susan Cain, *Quiet: The Power of Introverts in a World That Can't Stop Talking* (New York: Crown, 2012).

25. See, for instance, Table 1 in Wendy S. Dunn, Michael K. Mount, Murray R. Barrick, and Deniz S. Ones, "Relative Importance of Personality and General Mental Ability in Managers' Judgments of Applicant Qualifications," *Journal of Applied Psychology* 80, no. 4 (August 1995): 500–509.

26. Adrian Furnham and Carl Fudge, "The Five Factor Model of Personality and Sales Performance," *Journal of Individual Differences* 29, no. 1 (January 2008): 11–16; Murray R. Barrick, Michael K. Mount, and Judy P. Strauss, "Conscientiousness and Performance of Sales Representatives: Test of the Mediating Effects of Goal Setting," *Journal of Applied Psychology* 78, no. 5 (October 1993): 715–22 (emphasis added).

27. Murray R. Barrick, Michael K. Mount, and Timothy A. Judge, "Personality and Performance at the Beginning of the New Millennium: What Do We Know and Where Do We Go Next?" *International Journal of Selection and Assessment* 9, nos. 1–2 (March–June 2001): 9–30.

28. See, for instance, Adam M. Grant, Francesca Gino, and David A. Hofmann, "Reversing the Extraverted Leadership Advantage: The Role of Employee Proactivity," *Academy of Management Journal* 54, no. 3 (June 2011): 528–50.

29. Adam M. Grant, "Rethinking the Extraverted Sales Ideal: The Ambivert Advantage," *Psychological Science* (forthcoming, 2013).

30. H. J. Eysenck, *Readings in Extraversion and Introversion: Bearings on Basic Psychological Processes* (New York: Staples Press, 1971).

31. Grant, "Rethinking the Extraverted Sales Ideal."

32. Ibid.

33. Steve W. Martin, "Seven Personality Traits of Top Salespeople," *HBR Blog Network*, June 27, 2011, available at http://blogs.hbr.org/cs/2011/06/the_seven_personality _traits_o.html; Lynette J. Ryals and Iain Davies, "Do You Really Know Who Your Best Salespeople Are?" *Harvard Business Review*, December 2010.

34. Nate Boaz, John Murnane, and Kevin Nuffer, "The Basics of Business-to-Business Sales Success," *McKinsey Quarterly* (May 2010).

35. Cain, *Quiet: The Power of Introverts*, 166.

36. Deniz S. Ones and Stephan Dilchert, "How Special Are Executives? How Special Should Executive Selection Be? Observations and Recommendations," *Industrial and Organizational Psychology* 2, no. 2 (June 2009): 163–70.

CHAPTER 5. BUOYANCY

1. Og Mandino, *The Greatest Salesman in the World* (New York: Bantam, 1968), 71, 87.

2. Napoleon Hill, *How to Sell Your Way Through Life* (Hoboken, NJ: Wiley, 2010), 49.

3. Ibrahim Senay, Dolores Albarracín, and Kenji Noguchi, "Motivating Goal-Directed Behavior Through Introspective Self-Talk: The Role of the Interrogative Form of Simple Future Tense," *Psychological Science* 21, no. 4 (April 2010): 499–504.

4. Ibid., 500-501.

5. Ibid., 500.

6. See, in particular, the work of Edward L. Deci and Richard M. Ryan, for example, Edward L. Deci and Richard M. Ryan, "The 'What' and 'Why' of Goal Pursuits: Human Needs and the Self-Determination of Behavior," *Psychological Inquiry* 11, no. 4 (October 2000): 227–68. I describe some of this research in my own Daniel H. Pink, *Drive: The Surprising Truth About What Motivates Us* (New York: Riverhead Books, 2009).

7. Shirli Kopelman, Ashleigh Shelby Rosette, and Leigh Thompson, "The Three Faces of Eve: Strategic Displays of Positive, Negative, and Neutral Emotions in Negotiations," *Organizational Behavior and Human Decision Processes* 99, no. 1 (January 2006): 81–101.

8. Ibid.

9. Barbara L. Fredrickson, *Positivity: Top-Notch Research Reveals the 3 to 1 Ratio That Will Change Your Life* (New York: Three Rivers Press, 2009), 21.

10. Barbara L. Fredrickson and Marcial F. Losada, "Positive Affect and the Complex Dynamics of Human Flourishing," *American Psychologist* 60, no. 7 (October 2005): 678–86.

11. Cory R. Scherer and Brad J. Sagarin, "Indecent Influence: The Positive Effects of Obscenity on Persuasion," *Social Influence* 1, no. 2 (June 2006): 138–46.

12. See, for instance, Marcial Losada and Emily Heaphy, "The Role of Positivity and Connectivity in the Performance of Business Teams: A Nonlinear Dynamics Model," *American Behavioral Scientist* 47, no. 6 (February 2004): 740–65.

13. Fredrickson and Losada, "Positive Affect."

14. Ibid., 685.

15. Fredrickson, *Positivity*, 137.

16. Martin E. P. Seligman and Peter Schulman, "Explanatory Style as a Predictor of Productivity and Quitting Among Life Insurance Sales Agents," *Journal of Personality and Social Psychology* 50, no. 4 (April 1986): 832–38.

17. Martin E. P. Seligman, *Learned Optimism: How to Change Your Mind and Your Life* (New York: Vintage Books, 2006), 7, 8.

18. Seligman and Schulman, "Explanatory Style," 834–35.
19. Ibid., 835.
20. Seligman, *Learned Optimism,* 292.

CHAPTER 6. CLARITY

1. Alicia H. Munnell, Anthony Webb, Luke Delorme, and Francesca Golub-Saas, "National Retirement Risk Index: How Much Longer Do We Need to Work?" Center for Retirement Research Report, no. 12-12 (June 2012); Teresa Ghilarducci, "Our Ridiculous Approach to Retirement," *New York Times,* July 21, 2012.

2. See, for instance, Shane Frederick, Nathan Novemsky, Jing Wang, Ravi Rhar, and Stephen Nowlis, "Opportunity Cost Neglect," *Journal of Consumer Research* 36 (2009): 553–61.

3. Hal E. Hershfield, Daniel G. Goldstein, William F. Sharpe, Jesse Fox, Leo Yeykelis, Laura L. Carstensen, and Jeremy N. Bailenson, "Increasing Saving Behavior Through Age-Processed Renderings of the Future Self," *Journal of Marketing Research* 48 (2011): S23–S37.

4. Hershfield et al., "Increasing Saving Behavior."

5. Ibid., citing Hal Erner-Hershfield, M. Tess Garton, Kacey Ballard, Gregory R. Samanez-Larken, and Brian Knutson, "Don't Stop Thinking About Tomorrow: Individual Differences in Future-Self Continuity Account for Saving," *Judgment and Decision Making* 4 (2009): 280–86.

6. Hershfield et al., "Increasing Saving Behavior."

7. Jacob Getzels and Mihaly Csikszentmihalyi, *The Creative Vision: A Longitudinal Study of Problem Finding in Art* (New York: Wiley, 1976); Mihaly Csikszentmihalyi and Jacob Getzels, "Creativity and Problem Finding," in Frank H. Farley and Ronald W. Neperud, eds., *The Foundations of Aesthetics, Art, and Art Education* (New York: Praeger, 1988). The quotation itself appears in Mihaly Csikszentmihalyi, *Flow: The Psychology of Optimal Experience* (New York: Harper Perennial, 1981), 277.

8. J. W. Getzels, "Problem Finding: A Theoretical Note," *Cognitive Science* 3 (1979): 167–72.

9. See, for example, Herbert A. Simon, "Creativity and Motivation: A Response to Csikszentmihalyi," *New Ideas in Psychology* 6 (1989): 177–81; Stéphanie Z. Dudek and Rémi Cote, "Problem Finding Revisited," in Mark A. Runco, ed., *Problem Finding, Problem Solving, and Creativity* (Norwood, NJ: Ablex, 1994).

10. The Conference Board, *Ready to Innovate: Are Educators and Executives Aligned on the Creative Readiness of the U.S. Workforce?* Research Report R-1424-08-RR (October 2008), available at http://www.artsusa.org/pdf/information _services/research/policy_roundtable/readytoinnovatefull.pdf.

11. Robert B. Cialdini, *Influence: Science and Practice,* 5th ed. (Boston: Allyn & Bacon, 2009), 12–16.

12. For a good introduction, see Daniel Kahneman and Amos Tversky, "The Framing of Decisions and the Psychology of Choice," *Science* 211 (1981): 453–58; Daniel

Kahneman and Amos Tversky, "Rational Choice and the Framing of Decisions," in Robin M. Hogarth and Melvin W. Reder, eds., *Rational Choice: The Contrast Between Economics and Psychology* (Chicago: University of Chicago Press, 1987); Erving Goffman, *Frame Analysis: An Essay on the Organization of Experience* (Cambridge MA: Harvard University Press, 1974).

13. Sheena S. Iyengar and Mark R. Lepper, "When Choice Is Demotivating: Can One Desire Too Much of a Good Thing?" *Journal of Personality and Social Psychology* 79 (2000): 995–1006.

14. Aaron R. Brough and Alexander Chernev, "When Opposites Detract: Categorical Reasoning and Subtractive Valuations of Product Combinations," *Journal of Consumer Research* 39 (August 2012): 1–16, 13.

15. Leaf Van Boven and Thomas Gilovich, "To Do or to Have? That Is the Question," *Journal of Personality and Social Psychology* 85 (2003): 1193–1202, 1194.

16. Ibid.

17. Varda Liberman, Steven M. Samuels, and Lee Ross, "The Name of the Game: Predictive Power of Reputations Versus Situational Labels in Determining Prisoner's Dilemma Game Moves," *Personality and Social Psychology Bulletin* 30 (September 2004): 1175–85.

18. Danit Ein-Gar, Baba Shiv, and Zakary L. Tormala, "When Blemishing Leads to Blossoming: The Positive Effect of Negative Information," *Journal of Consumer Research* 38 (2012): 846–59.

19. Zakary Tormala, Jayson Jia, and Michael Norton, "The Preference for Potential," *Journal of Personality and Social Psychology* 103 (October 2012): 567–83.

20. This explanation is based on an account in Lee Ross and Richard E. Nisbett, *The Person and the Situation* (London: Pinter & Martin, 2011), 132–33.

CHAPTER 7. PITCH

1. For accounts of Otis and his invention, see Spencer Klaw, "All Safe, Gentlemen, All Safe!" *American Heritage* 29, no. 5 (August–September 1978); PBS Online, "Who Made America?" available at http://www.pbs.org/wgbh/theymadeamerica/whomade/otis_hi.html; Otis Worldwide, "About Elevators," available at http://www.otisworldwide.com/pdf/AboutElevators.pdf.

2. Kimberly D. Elsbach and Roderick M. Kramer, "Assessing Creativity in Hollywood Pitch Meetings: Evidence for a Dual-Process Model of Creativity Judgments," *Academy of Management Journal* 46, no. 3 (June 2003): 283–301.

3. Ibid., 294.

4. Kimberly D. Elsbach, "How to Pitch a Brilliant Idea," *Harvard Business Review* 81, no. 9 (September 2003): 117–23.

5. Elsbach and Kramer, "Assessing Creativity in Hollywood Pitch Meetings," 296.

6. "Wordy Goods," *Economist*, August 22, 2012, available at http://www.economist.com/blogs/graphicdetail/2012/08/daily-chart-5.

7. Maurice Saatchi, "The Strange Death of Modern Advertising," *Financial Times*, June 22, 2006.

8. Ibid.

9. Robert E. Burnkrant and Daniel J. Howard, "Effects of the Use of Introductory Rhetorical Questions Versus Statements on Information Processing," *Journal of Personality and Social Psychology* 47, no. 6 (December 1984): 1218–30. For somewhat similar findings, see Richard E. Petty, John T. Cacioppo, and Martin Heesacker, "Effects of Rhetorical Questions on Persuasion: A Cognitive Response Analysis," *Journal of Personality and Social Psychology* 40, no. 3 (March 1981): 432–40. For the role played by the asker, see Rohini Ahluwalia and Robert E. Burnkrant, "Answering Questions About Questions: A Persuasion Knowledge Perspective for Understanding the Effects of Rhetorical Questions," *Journal of Consumer Research* 31 (June 2004): 26–42.

10. Burnkrant and Howard, "Effects of the Use of Introductory Rhetorical Questions," 1224.

11. "CNN Poll: Are You Better Off Than Four Years Ago?" CNN.com, September 13, 2012, available at http://bit.ly/OKlUAy.

12. Matthew S. McGlone and Jessica Tofighbakhsh, "Birds of a Feather Flock Conjointly (?): Rhyme as Reason in Aphorisms," *Psychological Science* 11, no. 5 (September 2000): 424–28.

13. Ibid.

14. Nicolas Ducheneaut and Victoria Bellotti, "E-mail as Habitat: An Exploration of Embedded Personal Information Management," *ACM Interactions* 8, no. 5 (September–October 2001): 30–38.

15. Jaclyn Wainer, Laura Dabbish, and Robert Kraut, "Should I Open This Email? Inbox-Level Cues, Curiosity, and Attention to Email," Proceedings of the 2011 Annual Conference on Human Factors in Computing Systems, May 7–12, 2011, Vancouver, British Columbia, available at http://kraut.hciresearch.org/sites/kraut.hciresearch.org/files/articles/Dabbish11-EmailCuriosity.pdf.

16. Once again, the landmark work of Edward Deci and Richard Ryan is instructive. For an overview of their research, see their publications (http://selfdeterminationtheory.org/browse-publications) or my own, Daniel H. Pink, *Drive: The Surprising Truth About What Motivates Us* (New York: Riverhead Books, 2009).

17. Brian Clark, "The Three Key Elements of Irresistible Email Subject Lines," *Copyblogger*, August 26, 2010, available at http://www.copyblogger.com/email-subject-lines/.

18. Melissa Korn, "Tweets, Plays Well w/Others: A Perfect M.B.A. Candidate," *Wall Street Journal*, September 1, 2011; Ian Wylie, "Learning the Game of Social Media," *Financial Times*, September 5, 2011.

19. Sarah Perez, "Twitpitch: The Elevator Pitch Hits Twitter," *ReadWriteWeb*, April 18, 2008, available at http://www.readwriteweb.com/archives/twitpitch_the_elevator_pitch_hits_twitter.php.

20. Paul André, Michael S. Bernstein, and Kurt Luther, "Who Gives a Tweet?: Evaluating Microblog Content Value," paper presented at the 2012 ACM Conference on Computer Supported Co-operative Work, February 11–15, 2012, Seattle, Washington, available at http://www.cs.cmu.edu/~pandre/pubs/whogivesatweet-cscw2012.pdf.

21. Ibid. I've excluded the category "Conversation," in which tweeters make public their communication with others, because this category is less relevant to pitching.

22. André, Bernstein, and Luther, "Who Gives a Tweet?" See Figure 1 and Table 1.

23. "Pixar Movies at the Box Office," Box Office Mojo, available at http://boxofficemojo.com/franchises/chart/?id=pixar.htm.

24. "Pixar Story Rules (One Version)," *Pixar Touch Blog*, May 15, 2011, available at http://www.pixartouchbook.com/blog/2011/5/15/pixar-story-rules-one-version.html.

25. See, for instance, Jonathan Gottschall, *The Storytelling Animal: How Stories Make Us Human* (New York: Houghton Mifflin Harcourt, 2012), and Peter Guber, *Tell to Win: Connect, Persuade, and Triumph with the Hidden Power of Story* (New York: Crown Business, 2011).

CHAPTER 8. IMPROVISE

1. Walter A. Friedman, "John H. Patterson and the Sales Strategy of the National Cash Register Company, 1884 to 1922," *Business History Review* 72, no. 4 (Winter 1998): 552–84. If you're interested in the early evolution of sales in America, read Friedman's gem of a book, Walter A. Friedman, *Birth of a Salesman: The Transformation of Selling in America* (Cambridge, MA: Harvard University Press, 2004).

2. Walter A. Friedman, "John H. Patterson and the Sales Strategy of the National Cash Register Company, 1884 to 1922," *Harvard Business School Working Knowledge*, November 2, 1999, available at http://hbswk.hbs.edu/item/1143.html.

3. "The Lord Chamberlain & Censorship," *Leither Magazine*, March 9, 2012, available at http://www.leithermagazine.com/2012/03/09/the-lord-chamberlain-censorship.html.

4. See Mary M. Crossan, "Improvisation in Action," *Organization Science* 9, no. 5 (September–October 1998): 593–99; Dusya Vera and Mary Crossan, "Theatrical Improvisation: Lessons for Organizations," *Organization Studies* 25, no. 5 (June 2004): 727–49; Mary M. Crossan, João Vieira da Cunha, Miguel Pina E. Cunha, and Dusya Vera, "Time and Organizational Improvisation," *FEUNL Working Paper No. 410*, 2002, available at http://dx.doi.org/10.2139/ssrn.881839; Keith Sawyer, *Group Genius: The Creative Power of Collaboration* (New York: Basic Books, 2007); Patricia Ryan Madson, *Improv Wisdom: Don't Prepare, Just Show Up* (New York: Bell Tower, 2005).

5. Zazli Lily Wisker, "The Effect of Personality, Emotional Intelligence and Social Network Characteristics on Sales Performance: The Mediating Roles of Market Intelligence Use, Adaptive Selling Behaviour and Improvisation" (doctoral thesis, University of Waikato, New Zealand, 2011).

6. Laura Janusik and Andrew Wolvin, "24 Hours in a Day: A Listening Update to the Time Studies," paper presented at the meeting of the International Listening Association, Salem, Oregon, 2006.

7. Mortimer Adler, *How to Speak/How to Listen* (New York: Touchstone, 1997), 5.

8. Judith Lee, "10 Ways to Communicate Better with Patients," *Review of Ophthalmology* 7, no. 10 (October 2000): 38.

9. Keith Johnstone, *Impro: Improvisation and the Theatre* (New York: Routledge, 1981), 99.

10. Stephen R. Covey, *The 7 Habits of Highly Effective People* (New York: Free Press, 1990), 207.

11. Alfred C. Fuller (as told to Hartzell Spence), *A Foot in the Door: The Life Appraisal of the Original Fuller Brush Man* (New York: McGraw-Hill, 1960), 193.

CHAPTER 9. SERVE

1. World Health Organization, *Global Status Report on Road Safety*, 2009, available at http://whqlibdoc.who.int/publications/2009/9789241563840_eng.pdf. See Table A.2.

2. Ibid., 1, 2. See Table 1.

3. James Habyarimana and William Jack, "Heckle and Chide: Results of a Randomized Road Safety Intervention in Kenya," *Journal of Public Economics* 95, nos. 11–12 (December 2011): 1438–46.

4. Ibid., 441.

5. Ibid., 444.

6. Yehonatan Turner and Irith Hadas-Halpern, "The Effects of Including a Patient's Photograph to the Radiographic Examination," paper presented at Radiological Society of North America Ninety-fourth Scientific Assembly and Annual Meeting, December 3, 2008. See also "Patient Photos Spur Radiologist Empathy and Eye for Detail," RSNA Press Release, December 2, 2008; Dina Kraft, "Radiologist Adds a Human Touch: Photos," *New York Times*, April 7, 2009.

7. Turner and Hadas-Halpern, "The Effects of Including a Patient's Photograph."

8. "Patient Photos Spur Radiologist Empathy and Eye for Detail," *ScienceDaily*, December 14, 2008, available at http://bit.ly/JbbEQt.

9. See Atul Gawande, *The Checklist Manifesto: How to Get Things Right* (New York: Picador, 2011).

10. See, for instance, "Disconnection from Patients and Care Providers: A Latent Error in Pathology and Laboratory Medicine: An Interview with Stephen Raab, MD," *Clinical Laboratory News* 35, no. 4 (April 2009).

11. Sally Herships, "The Power of a Simple 'Thank You,'" *Marketplace Radio*, December 22, 2010.

12. R. Douglas Scott II, *The Direct Medical Costs of Healthcare-Associated Infections in U.S. Hospitals and the Benefits of Prevention*, Centers for Disease Control and Prevention, March 2009, available at http://www.cdc.gov/HAI/pdfs/hai/Scott _CostPaper.pdf; Andrew Pollack, "Rising Threat of Infections Unfazed by Antibiotics," *New York Times*, February 26, 2010; R. Monina Klevens et al., "Estimating Health Care–Associated Infections and Deaths in U.S. Hospitals, 2002," *Public Health Reports* 122, no. 2 (March–April 2007): 160–66.

13. Adam M. Grant and David A. Hofmann, "It's Not All About Me: Motivating

Hand Hygiene Among Health Care Professionals by Focusing on Patients," *Psychological Science* 22, no. 12 (December 2011): 1494–99.

14. Ibid., 497.

15. Atul Gawande, "The Checklist," *New Yorker*, December 10, 2007; Gawande, *The Checklist Manifesto: How to Get Things Done Right* (New York: Picador, 2011).

16. Grant and Hofmann, "It's Not All About Me," 498.

17. See, for instance, Dan Ariely, Anat Bracha, and Stephan Meier, "Doing Good or Doing Well? Image Motivation and Monetary Incentives in Behaving Prosocially," *American Economic Review* 99, no. 1 (March 2009): 544–55; Stephan Meier, *The Economics of Non-Selfish Behaviour: Decisions to Contribute Money to Public Goods* (Cheltenham, UK: Edward Elgar Publishing Limited, 2006); Stephan Meier, "A Survey of Economic Theories and Field Evidence on Pro-Social Behavior," in Bruno S. Frey and Alois Stutzer, eds., *Economics and Psychology: A Promising New Cross-Disciplinary Field* (Cambridge, MA: MIT Press, 2007), 51–88.

18. Laurel Evans, Gregory R. Maio, Adam Corner, Carl J. Hodgetts, Sameera Ahmed, and Ulrike Hahn, "Self-Interest and Pro-Environmental Behaviour," *Nature Climate Change*, published online August 12, 2012, available at http://dx.doi.org/10.1038/nclimate1662.

19. Adam M. Grant, "The Significance of Task Significance: Job Performance Effects, Relational Mechanisms, and Boundary Conditions," *Journal of Applied Psychology* 93, no. 1 (2008): 108–24.

20. Robert K. Greenleaf, *Servant Leadership: A Journey into the Nature of Legitimate Power and Greatness, 25th Anniversary Edition* (Mahwah, NJ: Paulist Press, 2002), 27.

21. Ibid.

22. Alfred C. Fuller (as told to Hartzell Spence), *A Foot in the Door: The Life Appraisal of the Original Fuller Brush Man* (New York: McGraw-Hill, 1960), 87.

Index

Index